CARL A. RUDISILL LIBRARY
LENOIR-RHYNE COLLEGE

GAYLORD

The QUINTESSENTIAL QUIZBOOK

Being a Compendium of Curious Words,
Derivations, Literary Allusions, and
Little-Known Oddities of Fact and Fiction

by Norman G. Hickman

CARL A. RUDISILL LIBRARY
LENOIR-RHYNE COLLEGE

ST. MARTIN'S PRESS
NEW YORK

*AG
195
.H52
1979
June 1998*

Copyright © 1979 by Norman G. Hickman
All rights reserved. For information, write:
St. Martin's Press, Inc., 175 Fifth Ave., New York, N.Y. 10010.
Manufactured in the United States of America

Library of Congress Cataloging in Publication Data
Hickman, Norman, G.
  The quintessential quiz book.

  1. Questions and answers. I. Title.
AG195.H52—031′.02—78-21415
ISBN 0-312-66119-3

CONTENTS

The greatest part of a writer's time is spent in reading, in order to write: a man will turn over half a library to make one book.

—Dr. Samuel Johnson,
according to James Boswell

For my dear wife Minnie,
the quintessential researcher

ACKNOWLEDGMENTS

I am very grateful to those who have taken the trouble to read these pages in whole or in part and who have made invaluable suggestions: Julie Allen, Helen and Stanley Barnes, Roy Bartolomei, Pat Birch Becker, Anthony Montague Browne, Rear Admiral John D. Bulkeley, USN, Doris Bullard, Allan C. Butler, Andrew Carduner, Alexander Cassatt, Jr., Julia Child, Richard Coulson, Peter Duchin, Ahmet M. Ertegun, Douglas Fairbanks, Jr., Ronald Fieve, M.D., Judith Frank, Eugene Gonzales, Mark Goodson, Julie Gould, Charles Green, John Hammond, Center Hitchcock, Harold K. Hochschild, Francis T. Hunter, Florence Jensen, Alfred Kazin, Peter Kriendler, Peter Morrell, Coleman W. Morton, Patricia Munn, Dan Nooger, Julio Noyes, Thomas W. Phipps, Arthur Prager, Edgar Alsop Riley, M.D., Bonnie Rothbart, Jerome Shaw, Father Arthur Smith, OSA, Sheldon Tannen, Pamela Timmins, John Train, Nancy Tuckerman, Frank C. Waldrop, Frederick S. Wildman, Jr., Max Wilk, and Kristi Witken.

I wish to acknowledge the help given me by Leslie Pockell, my editor, and Paula Reedy in coping with a too copious author.

For Roz Cole, who said, "Why don't you write a book?" I am thankful for the chance to exercise what God has given to Man . . . a curiosity.

Special thanks are due to Timothy Dickinson, contributing editor of *Harper's* magazine, whose fund of esoterica might even baffle the formidable Dr. Johnson. Finally, let me express my gratitude to Anne Morea for preparing the typescript with such skill and judgment.

Thanks are due for permission to reprint from the following copyright material:

Belloc, Hilaire, "On A Sundial" and "On His Books", *Sonnets and Verse.* (London: Gerald Duckworth & Co., Ltd.). Reprinted by permission of A.D. Peters & Co., Ltd., London.

Burnam, Tom, from *The Dictionary of Misinformation.* (New York: Harper & Row, 1975). Reprinted by permission of Harper & Row Publishers, Inc.

Churchill, Winston S., from *Painting as a Pastime.* (London: Ernest Benn, Ltd.). Reprinted by permission of Ernest Benn, Ltd.

Churchill, Winston S., from *My Early Life: A Roving Commission.* (New York: Charles Scribner's Sons, 1930). Reprinted by permission of Charles Scribner's Sons.

Eliot, T.S., "Macavity", *Old Possum's Book of Practical Cats* and "The Hollow Men", *Collected Poems 1909–1962.* (New York: Harcourt Brace Jovanovich, Inc., 1968). Reprinted by permission of Harcourt Brace Jovanovich, Inc.

Espy, Willard R., from *Mr. Anonymous.* (New York: Clarkson N. Potter, Inc.). Reprinted by permission of Willard R. Espy.

Herbert, A.P., from *Lines on a Book Borrowed from the Ship's Doctor.* Reprinted by permission of the Estate of the late A.P. Herbert and A.P. Watt, Ltd.

Housman, A.E., "When I Was One and Twenty" and "A Shropshire Lad", from authorized editions of *The Collected Poems of A.E. Housman.* (New York: Holt, Rinehart & Winston, 1939, 1940, 1965. Copyright 1967–68 by Robert E. Symons). Reprinted by permission of Holt, Rinehart & Winston.

Macroff, Gene I., "Spelldown", *The New York Times,* August 4, 1973. (New York: The New York Times Commpany, 1973). Reprinted in the March, 1974 issue of *Reader's Digest.*

Nash, Ogden. "The Pig", "The Turtle", "Reflections on Ice-Breaking", *Verses From 1929 On.* (New York: Little, Brown & Co., 1933, 1940, 1930). Reprinted by permission of Little, Brown & Co.

Perelman, S.J., "Kitchen Bouquet", *The Most of S.J. Perelman.* (New York: Simon & Schuster, a Division of Gulf & Western Corp., 1930–58). Reprinted by permission of Simon & Schuster.

Schieckele, Peter, *The Definitive Biography of P.D.Q. Bach.* (New York: Random House, Inc., 1976). Reprinted by permission of Random House, Inc.

Thurber, James. Reprinted by permission of Mrs. James Thurber for two cartoon captions copyright 1943 by James Thurber. Renewed 1971. From *Men, Women and Dogs,* published by Harcourt Brace Jovanovich. Originally printed in *The New Yorker.*

Zern, Ed, "Exit Laughing", *Field and Stream.* Reprinted by permission of *Field and Stream.*

BEGINNINGS

1. What is the first verse in the Bible?
2. Which famous play begins with this line?

   "If music be the food of love, play on."
3. Name the first state to ratify the Constitution.
4. Who gave us "Begin the Beguine"?
5. Which well-known novel starts as follows?

   It was the best of times, it was the worst of times, it was the age of wisdom, it was the age of foolishness, it was the epoch of belief, it was the epoch of incredulity, it was the season of Light, it was the season of Darkness, it was the spring of hope, it was the winter of despair.
6. In which play is "the beginning of fairies" explained?
7. "Last night I dreamt I went to Manderley again" is the opening sentence of which novel?
8. According to the Bible, what is "the beginning of wisdom"?
9. Who wrote the following lines?

   From quiet homes and first beginning,
   Out to the undiscovered ends,
   There's nothing worth the wear of winning,
   But laughter and the love of friends.
10. On what turning point in World War II did a nation's leader speak as follows?

    Now this is not the end. It is not even the beginning of the end. But it is, perhaps, the end of the beginning.

BEGINNINGS

1. "In the beginning God created the heaven and the earth."
   —Genesis 1:1
2. *Twelfth Night*, by William Shakespeare.
3. Delaware, in 1787.
4. Cole Porter.
5. *A Tale of Two Cities*, by Charles Dickens.
6. *Peter Pan*, by Sir James Barrie. "When the first baby laughed for the first time, the laugh broke into a thousand pieces and they all went skipping about, and that was the beginning of fairies."
7. *Rebecca*, by Daphne du Maurier.
8. "The fear of the Lord."—Psalms 111:10
9. Hilaire Belloc, "Dedicatory Ode."
10. Winston Churchill, in a speech at the Lord Mayor's Day luncheon in London, November 1942, following the decisive British victory at El Alamein in World War II.

ABBREVIATIONS

What do the following mean?

1. K.C.B.
2. I.N.R.I.
3. C.C.C.P.
4. D.V.M.
5. a.k.a.
6. F.F.V.
7. b.i.d.
8. Q.E.D.
9. N.O.C.D.
10. AWOL

ABBREVIATIONS

1. Knight Commander of the Bath.
2. Jesus the Nazarene, King of the Jews (Latin *Iesus Nazarenus Rex Iudaeorum*).
3. U.S.S.R. In the Russian alphabet *C* is equivalent to the English *S*, and *P* to the English *R*. Thus C.C.C.P. in the English alphabet reads *Soiuz Sovetskikh Sotsialisticheskikh Respublik*.
4. Doctor of Veterinary Medicine.
5. also known as.
6. First Families of Virginia, self-styled leaders of Southern aristocracy.
7. twice a day (Latin *bis in die*)—generally used by doctors on prescriptions. "t.i.d." is three times a day.
8. That which was to be demonstrated or proved (Latin *quod erat demonstrandum*). Q.E.D. is generally used to indicate the solution of geometric problems.
9. Not our class, dear.
10. Absent without leave. (Although *without* is one word, to abbreviate this phrase without the *O* would mean "absent *with* leave.")

ACRONYMS

An acronym is a word formed from the initial letters of a name or by combining initial letters or parts of a series of words. How many of the following can you "translate"?

1. RADAR
2. SCUBA
3. FLAK
4. QANTAS
5. LASER
6. GESTAPO
7. IATA
8. SNAFU
9. SWAK
10. FASGROLIA

ACRONYMS

1. *Radio Detecting And Ranging*
2. *Self-Contained Underwater Breathing Apparatus*
3. *Flieger Abwehr Kanone* (aircraft defense gun)
4. *Queensland and Northern Territory Aerial Services*
5. *Light Amplification by Stimulated Emission of Radiation*
6. *Geheime Staatspolizei* (Secret State Police)
7. *International Air Transport Association*
8. *Situation Normal: All Fucked Up*
9. *Sealed With A Kiss*
10. *Fast Growing Language of Initials and Acronyms*

ALIASES

Can you give the real names of the following?

ALIASES

1. Mary Ann Evans.
2. Vladimir Ilyich Ulyanov.
3. Domenicos Theotocopoulos.
4. Hector Hugh Munro, who took the name "Saki" from the cup-bearer in the *Rubáiyát of Omar Khayyám*.
5. Charles Dickens. Boz was the nickname of his younger brother.
6. Charles Lutwidge Dodgson, a mathematician at Oxford, where he wrote *Euclid and His Modern Rivals*.
7. Agatha Christie, who was married to the archaeologist Sir Max Mallowan, used the name Mary Westmacott for her romantic novels.
8. Oscar Wilde used the name Sebastian Melmoth after his release from Reading Gaol. He chose Sebastian because of the arrows on the prison uniforms; Melmoth because one of his mother's kinsmen had written *Melmoth the Wanderer,* a famous novel of a man who had sold his soul.
9. William Sydney Porter, who spent three years in the Ohio Penitentiary for embezzlement. While there, he began writing short stories under a variety of pen names, including Oliver Henry, which later evolved into O. Henry.
10. Hitler, not Schicklgrüber. Hitler's grandmother was an unwed mother named Maria Anna Schicklgrüber. On the birth certificate of her son, Alois, the space for the father's name was left blank, and Alois went by the name Schicklgrüber until he was in his thirties. Before his son, Adolf, was born, though, Alois changed his name to Hitler, which was a variant of Heidler, the name of the man Maria Anna Schicklgrüber eventually married.

AMERICAN HISTORY

1. Can you name Columbus' first landfall?
2. Where was the first permanent English settlement in North America?
3. Which hero of an important battle in the Revolution has been accorded a statue that does not bear his name? Where is it located?
4. Which general, who later became president, won a decisive victory after the war was over?
5. What took place in Philadelphia on July 4, 1776?
6. Do you know the two essential points of the Monroe Doctrine?
7. Against which president were impeachment proceedings brought?
8. Which Chief Justice did most by his decisions to fix the interpretation of the U.S. Constitution?
9. Who was the first woman nominated for the presidency?
10. Who made the decision to use the atomic bomb?

AMERICAN HISTORY

1. San Salvador Island, also known as Watlings Island, in the Bahamas.
2. Jamestown, Virginia, in 1607.
3. Benedict Arnold, in Saratoga. His name is omitted because of his later betrayal of his country.
4. Andrew Jackson, who defeated the British at New Orleans in the War of 1812 after peace had been signed in Europe.
5. The final draft of the Declaration of Independence was adopted, but not signed. The document was then engrossed on parchment, and all but six of the signatures were affixed on August 2, 1776.
6. The United States would not interfere in European affairs and would view with displeasure any attempt by European powers to extend their political influence over the nations of the New World.
7. Andrew Johnson.
8. John Marshall.
9. Victoria Woodhull, in 1872, by the People's Party, representing extreme radical organizations. She took the somewhat contradictory stand of favoring free love but not abortion. She had a sister named Tennessee Claflin, who was a bigger nut than she was.
10. Harry S. Truman. (The *S* in his name does not stand for anything.)

AMERICAN LITERATURE

1. Which American classic is subtitled *Life in the Woods*?
2. Who wrote *The Man Without a Country*, and who was the leading figure in the story?
3. What and where is Sunnyside?
4. Who offered this bit of literary criticism? What is the raven's name?

   > There comes Poe, with his raven, like Barnaby Rudge.
   > Three-fifths of him genius and two-fifths sheer fudge.

5. Which organization awards the Edgar, and for whom is it named?
6. In Fitzgerald's *The Great Gatsby*, where did Jay Gatsby give his fabulous parties?
7. Which famous fictional heroine was married to Charles Hamilton and Frank Kennedy?
8. Who is reputed to have directed that ten per cent of her ashes be sent to her agent?
9. In *The Gift of the Magi*, by O. Henry, what gifts were exchanged?
10. Who wrote these lines?

    > There is no Frigate like a Book
    > To take us Lands away
    > Nor any Coursers like a Page
    > Of prancing Poetry.

AMERICAN LITERATURE

1. *Walden*, by Henry David Thoreau.
2. Edward Everett Hale. Philip Nolan.
3. Washington Irving's country estate on the Hudson River near Tarrytown, New York. The surrounding region is described in his *Legend of Sleepy Hollow*.
4. James Russell Lowell in "A Fable for Cities." The name of Barnaby Rudge's raven is Grip.
5. The Mystery Writers of America give it for the best mystery of the year. Edgar Allan Poe.
6. At his mansion in West Egg, Long Island, outside of New York. West Egg is a fictitious name, but the location corresponds to Sands Point or Great Neck.
7. Scarlett O'Hara in Margaret Mitchell's *Gone With The Wind*.
8. Dorothy Parker.
9. Jim sold his watch to buy his wife, Della, a pair of tortoise-shell combs for her long, beautiful hair, while Della sold her hair to buy Jim a platinum fob chain for his watch.
10. Emily Dickinson, No. 1263. (*The Complete Poems*)

THE ANCIENT WORLD

1. Can you name five of the Seven Wonders of the ancient world?
2. Where are the Pillars of Hercules?
3. Explain the origin of the suffix "-chester" in place names such as Rochester and Winchester.
4. The name of the city of London had what ancient origins?
5. Ultima Thule was the name given by the Romans to a land north of Britain, which is believed to be what today?
6. Why might we consider Naples a new city?
7. The little yellow finch known as the canary takes its name from the Canary Islands, where these birds abound, but to what do the islands owe their name?
8. The land which Plato first described as "The Lost Atlantis" is now believed to be where?
9. The ancient Greeks considered themselves descended from a mythical Hellen and called their land Hellas. How did the name Greece come about?
10. The beginning of what is now Paris was an island in the Seine which the Romans called Lutetia. How did the name Paris come into being?

13

THE ANCIENT WORLD

1. The Great Pyramid of Cheops (Egypt), the Hanging Gardens of Babylon (Iraq), the Tomb of King Mausolus at Halicanrassus (Turkey), the Temple of Artemis at Ephesus (Turkey), the Colossus of Rhodes (the Isle of Rhodes in the Aegean), the Statue of Zeus at Olympia (Greece), and the lighthouse on the Isle of Pharos (off Alexandria, Egypt).

2. Promontories flanking the east entrance to the Straits of Gibraltar.

3. When the Romans occupied Britain, they had to build fortified camps, which they called *castra*, to hold the island. As settlements became established, the Roman *castra* became incorporated with the older Celtic names and in time became the suffixes -caster, -cester, or -chester.

4. The original British settlement on the site was *Londinion*. The Romans changed the ending to the Latin *Londinium*, and when they left, the Anglo-Saxons used no ending at all.

5. Iceland.

6. Because when the Greeks first settled there, they called it *Neapolis*, meaning "new town." This later became *Napoli,* and Naples in English.

7. To the Romans who, when they first landed there, were so amazed at the number of wild dogs that they named the land *canaria insula*, "the island of the dogs."

8. The Greek island of Thíra, or Santorin, in the Aegean.

9. The *Graikoi* or, in Latin, *Graeci*, were the first Hellenic tribe the Romans encountered in the western part of Hellas. They proceeded to use this tribal name for the whole country so that now the land is known as Greece.

10. Since the tribe that inhabited the island were known to the Romans as the Parisii, they called the settlement *Lutetia Parisiorum*, or Lutetia of the Parisians. Over the years the shortened name Paris was adopted for the city.

ANIMALS

1. The word *animal* is ultimately derived from the Latin word *anima*, which means what?
2. Who wrote a description of a farm on which men and pigs become indistinguishable?
3. A camelopard is an archaic term for what?
4. Can you give the common Swahili word for lion?
5. *Nanook*, in the Eskimo tongue, is what?
6. What kind of animal was Bagheera, and whom did he teach?
7. Give the correct term for the American buffalo.
8. What does a pangolin eat?
9. The skin of what animal is called Hudson Seal by furriers?
10. Can you name the author of the following?

> The pig, if I am not mistaken,
> Supplies us sausage, ham and bacon.
> Let others say his heart is big,
> I call it stupid of the pig.

15

ANIMALS

1. Breath.
2. George Orwell, in *Animal Farm*.
3. A giraffe, since it has a head like a camel's, and the spots of a leopard.
4. *Simba*.
5. A polar bear.
6. A black panther. Mowgli. (*The Jungle Book*, by Rudyard Kipling.)
7. The American bison.
8. Ants—it is a scaly anteater.
9. The muskrat.
10. Ogden Nash, "The Pig," from *Happy Days*.

16

ARCHAEOLOGY

1. Name the three ages which are commonly used in archaeological study.
2. Explain the importance of the Rosetta Stone, which was discovered in Egypt by Napoleon's troops in 1799 and is now in the British Museum.
3. With which areas of excavation are the archaeologists Heinrich Schliemann and Sir Arthur Evans associated?
4. What is Stonehenge and where is it located?
5. Who in 1922 discovered the fabulous tomb of King Tutankhamun in the Valley of the Kings, near Luxor, and who was his patron?
6. Can you describe a barrow and a kitchen midden?
7. In the eruption of Mt. Vesuvius in A.D. 79, what was Pompeii covered with?
8. Name the supreme example of the Khmer temple building which was the meeting place of gods and kings and the deities' earthly home.
9. Which extraordinary ruin was discovered in 1911 by the American explorer Hiram Bingham?
10. Who in this century located in the Olduvai Gorge, Tanzania, a hominid fossil dating back over 1.7 million years?

ARCHAEOLOGY

1. The Stone, Bronze, and Iron Ages, referring to the material from which weapons and implements were made.
2. The Rosetta Stone, a basalt tablet with a decree of Ptolemy V written in Greek, Egyptian hieroglyphic, and demotic (a simplified form of ancient Egyptian hieratic writing), provided the key to deciphering hieroglyphics by Champollion and others.
3. Schliemann with Troy and Greece, Evans with Crete.
4. Stonehenge is a circular prehistoric ruin on the Salisbury Plain, Wiltshire, England, consisting of massive standing stones and lintels. Archaeologists are agreed that it served some sort of religious function, but it has also been theorized that it was used as an immense astronomical instrument.
5. Howard Carter. The fifth Earl of Carnarvon.
6. A barrow is a burial mound usually covered with earth, while a kitchen midden is a prehistoric refuse dump containing shells, bones, and artifacts.
7. Cinders and ashes, not lava.
8. Angkor Wat, in Cambodia. It is probably the largest religious structure in the world.
9. Machu Picchu, the fortress city of the ancient Incas, located high in the Peruvian Andes.
10. Dr. Mary D. Leakey, wife of the famous archaeologist and anthropologist, Dr. Louis Leakey, and mother of anthropologist Richard E. Leakey.

ASTROLOGY

1. Give the first and last signs of the zodiac, and the number of degrees in each sign. What is considered to be New Year's Day in astrology?
2. Why is the word *zodiac* a misnomer?
3. Which astronomer put astrology into a temporary eclipse?
4. In addition to the signs, the zodiac is divided into what the ancients considered the four great elements of air, fire, water, and earth. Do you know the astrological triplicities of these elements?
5. Who observed that "the fault . . . lies not in the stars, but in ourselves, that we are underlings"?
6. Which is the highest and most developed mental sign in the zodiac?
7. What is meant by the cusps?
8. Which sign represents the sexual or procreative element of man?
9. To cast your own horoscope is really quite simple. All you need is what?
10. Which group, in 1975, issued a statement saying that astrology has no basis in fact and contributes dangerously to "the cult of irrationalism and obscurantism"?

ASTROLOGY

1. Aries and Pisces. Thirty degrees. March 21.
2. Zodiac means "ring of animals," yet there are four human signs represented—Gemini the Twins, Virgo the Virgin, Sagittarius the Archer, and Aquarius the Water Bearer—and one object, Libra the Scales.
3. Nicholas Copernicus, the sixteenth-century Polish astronomer who proved that the sun was the center of our system and that the earth was one of the planets that revolved around it. Before this, astrologers had based their calculations on the Ptolemaic System, which held that the earth was the center, with the sun revolving around it. Understandably, astrology fell into great disfavor following Copernicus' discovery.
4. Air: Gemini, Libra, and Aquarius. Fire: Aries, Leo, and Sagittarius. Water: Cancer, Scorpio, and Pisces. Earth: Taurus, Virgo, and Capricorn.
5. Cassius in Shakespeare's *Julius Caesar*.
6. Aquarius, the symbol of which is waves, which represent not water, as is generally thought, but electricity or vibration. These waves are also referred to as parallel lines of force.
7. Cusps (Latin *cuspis*, point) are the transitional first and last parts of a house or sign.
8. Scorpio.
9. To cast your own horoscope you will need the following:
   a) A blank horoscope map b) Your date, hour, and place of birth c) An atlas, to determine the exact latitude and longitude of your birthplace d) An ephemeris, a book giving the places of the planets on your birthday e) A table of houses, giving the position and degrees of the signs f) An aspect finder, giving the configuration of the stars and planets in relation to one another and to you g) A book with interpretations of aspects and planetary positions.

   To go through all this, you just have to believe in astrology.
10. Eighteen Nobel laureates.

AUTOMOBILES

1. What new development transformed the manufacturing of automobiles?
2. Which country is credited with producing the first successful motorcars?
3. The phrase "flying teapot" was affectionately given to which early automobile?
4. In 1908 the first transcontinental automobile race, sponsored by *The New York Times* and *Le Matin* of Paris, started out from New York City, with four nations and six automobiles competing. The car from which country reached Paris first, and in what approximate time?
5. If a country banned all colors except pink for automobiles, what would it be?
6. What part did Mercedes have in the production of Mercedes-Benz cars?
7. Which two manufacturers each gave their names to two makes of automobiles?
8. What does drag racing involve?
9. Name the car which was introduced with great fanfare and became the flop of the fifties.
10. What are the fastest production road cars?

AUTOMOBILES

1. The internal-combustion engine.
2. Germany. In 1885 both Karl Benz, and Gottlieb Daimler, patented cars of this type. This was almost ten years before the first automobile, the Duryea, was made in the United States.
3. The Stanley Steamer, a steam-powered vehicle.
4. The American Thomas Flyer won the race, covering 13,340 miles in 169 days. Italy's Zust reached Paris two weeks later. Only one other car finished.
5. A pink car nation.
6. None at all. She was the daughter of Emil Jellinek, an Austrian, who named his racing cars after her. When Benz and Daimler merged in 1926, the new firm used the name.
7. From Ranson E. Olds we got the Reo and the Oldsmobile; from Henry J. Kaiser, the Henry J. (the first American small car, introduced after World War II) and the Kaiser-Fraser. Only the Oldsmobile is still being made.
8. Acceleration tests with extremely powerful cars over a quarter-mile track.
9. The Edsel, named after the son of Henry Ford, Sr.
10. The Lamborghini Countach P400 and the Ferrari BB Berlinetta Boxer.

BASEBALL AND FOOTBALL

1. From which two English games is baseball derived?
2. The oldest collegiate football series started between which two teams?
3. What were the real names of the "Georgia Peach" and the "Galloping Ghost"?
4. Name the coach who popularized the forward pass, developed the precision backfield or shift, and fielded the "Four Horsemen," the most famous backfield of all time.
5. Which famous sportswriter named the "Four Horsemen" and also wrote, ". . . not that you won or lost—but how you played the game"?
6. The phrase "Tinker to Evers to Chance" refers to whom?
7. In the film *The Graduate* what was the refrain in the song "Mrs. Robinson" that evoked the country's search for lost heroes?
8. Who has scored the most touchdowns (23) and also gained the greatest number of yards (2,003) in one season?
9. Give within twenty the home run record of Hank Aaron when he retired in 1976.
10. Why is there no joy in Mudville?

BASEBALL AND FOOTBALL

1. Cricket and the children's game of rounders.
2. Princeton and Rutgers. Their first game was played in 1869.
3. Ty Cobb and Red Grange.
4. Knute Rockne, head coach at Notre Dame from 1918 to 1931. The "Four Horsemen" were Harry Stuhldreher, Don Miller, Jim Crowley, and Elmer Layden.
5. Grantland Rice.
6. Three members of the Chicago Cubs' infield who were renowned for their ability to make double plays in the early years of this century.
7. "Where have you gone, Joe diMaggio?"
8. O.J. Simpson.
9. 755, beating Babe Ruth's record of 714 home runs.
10. For the reason given in this stanza from "Casey at the Bat", by Ernest Lawrence Thayer:

    Oh! somewhere in this favored land the sun is shining bright;
    The band is playing somewhere, and somewhere hearts are
        light;
    And somewhere men are laughing and somewhere children
        shout,
    But there is no joy in Mudville—mighty Casey has struck out.

BATHROOM AND BOUDOIR

1. The word *boudoir* comes from the French word *bouder*, which means what?
2. What do women use that means in Latin "to float through the air like smoke"?
3. If you were walking on the streets of old Edinburgh, why would the cry of "gardy-loo" be alarming?
4. Of what is castile soap supposed to be made?
5. A bidet is a basinlike fixture designed to be straddled for bathing the genitals and the posterior. What does the word mean in French?
6. Which mistress of Louis XV of France gave her name to a distinctive type of hair arrangement?
7. What is kohl, and for what is it used in Moslem and Asian countries?
8. What was Thomas Crapper's contribution to bathroom efficiency?
9. Can you describe a merkin?
10. Which is the stronger, toilet water or cologne?

BATHROOM AND BOUDOIR

1. To pout. The boudoir, then, is literally the pouting room.
2. Perfume, from the Latin *per-*, meaning through, and *fumus*, meaning smoke.
3. It was a cry, taken from the French, that slops were being emptied out of an upstairs window, the loo being a corruption of the French *l'eau*, meaning water.
4. Olive oil.
5. Trotter, a little horse.
6. Madame de Pompadour.
7. A preparation, made from powdered antimony, used by women to darken the edges of the eyelids.
8. He made the flush toilet possible through his invention of the valve-and-siphon arrangement. His firm has four royal warrants permitting it to advertise "By Appointment to Her Majesty the Queen." Thomas Crapper's biography is appropriately titled *Flushed With Pride.*
9. It is a hairpiece for a woman's pubic hair.
10. Toilet water.

THE BIBLE

1. Name the first five books of the Old Testament.
2. Of what were Adam and Eve forbidden to eat in the Garden of Eden?
3. What is the shortest verse in the Bible?
4. In the Parable of the Ten Virgins, what were the five foolish virgins guilty of neglecting?
5. Four words appeared on the wall at Belshazzar's feast. What were they, and what did they signify?
6. In Biblical usage, what can the verb "know" signify?
7. When "the voice of the turtle is heard in our land," what time of year is it, and what is the turtle?
8. According to the Bible, how many wise men, or Magi, came from the east to Jerusalem to see the newborn Jesus?
9. Where did Noah's ark come to rest?
10. Who was given custody of the body of Jesus following the crucifixion?

THE BIBLE

1. Genesis, Exodus, Leviticus, Numbers, Deuteronomy.
2. "Of the tree of the knowledge of good and evil." (Genisis 2:17).
3. "Jesus wept."—John 11:35.
4. They did not fill their lamps with oil. Hence, they could not welcome the wedding party and had to go forth into the darkness. The parable teaches the lesson of spiritual preparedness.
5. *Mene, mene, tekel, upharsin,* which are Aramaic words meaning "numbered, numbered, weighed, divided." (Daniel 5:25) Daniel interpreted the phrase to mean that God had doomed Belshazzar's kingdom.
6. To have carnal knowledge of, to have sexual intercourse with.
7. Spring. The turtledove.
8. There is no number given. Matthew 2:1 simply says, ". . . there came wise men from the east to Jerusalem." Christian tradition, however, has elaborated upon the biblical account: it has set their number as three, perhaps from their gifts of gold, frankincense, and myrrh; it has called them kings; and it has given them names: Caspar, Melchior, and Balthazar.
9. Not on Mount Ararat, but, according to Genesis 8:4, on "the mountains of Ararat," the reference being probably to the mountain range rather than to any particular peak.
10. Joseph of Arimathea. According to legend, he founded the first Christian Church in England at Glastonbury.

BIG AND LITTLE

1. Frances Hodgson Burnett devoted herself to the peerage in which novel?
2. Name two islands that are separated by an international boundary line and the international date line.
3. Which keen archer had a stature that belied his nickname?
4. Big Bertha, the large cannon used by the Germans in World War I, was named for whom?
5. Who observed that one would have to have a heart of stone to read about the death of Little Nell without laughing?
6. What is the more familiar name of a cluster of seven stars also known as the "Plow," the "Wain," and the "Wagon"?
7. Do you know the location of a section of the United States which is known as Little Egypt because of its delta?
8. Who created the enigmatic Chinese detective Charlie Chan?
9. Why did Fats Waller hate someone?
10. What was the name of the Antarctic base that Richard E. Byrd established in 1929?

BIG AND LITTLE

1. *Little Lord Fauntleroy*.
2. Big Diomede and Little Diomede, which lie in the Bering Strait between the U.S.S.R. and the United States.
3. Little John, in the legends about Robin Hood.
4. Bertha Krupp von Bohlen und Halbach, proprietress of the Krupp Works, where the cannon was made. (The German term was *dicke Bertha*, or Fat Bertha.)
5. Mark Twain.
6. The Big Dipper.
7. The deltalike region of Illinois, formed by the junction of the Ohio and Mississippi Rivers. There you will find towns with such names as Cairo, Karnak, and Thebes.
8. Earl Derr Biggers.
9. "I hates you, 'cause yo' feet's too big."
10. Little America.

BIRDS

1. What famous comic poet wrote *The Birds*?
2. What "perched upon a bust of Pallas just above my chamber door," and what did it say?
3. What is the only bird that provides us with leather?
4. Who wrote the following to whom?

   Hail to thee, blithe spirit!
   Bird thou never wert.

5. Can you explain the connection between the goose and the soft, sheer, gauzy fabric known as gossamer?
6. Which unpleasant bird often hunts when he is not hungry and impales his prey on long, sharp thorns to keep it in reserve for a rainy day?
7. Which bird, with the largest wing span of any living bird, was prominent in what famous poem by whom?
8. How did the shitepoke, a variety of North American heron, get its name?
9. Why is it illegal to shoot swans on the River Thames in England?
10. Collective nouns, as applied to birds and beasts, were first used in the sport of venery (used here in the sense of hunting, not lechery). How many of the following blanks can you fill in with the correct noun of assembly?

    a) A_____of quail
    b) A_____of peacocks
    c) A_____of finches
    d) A_____of starlings
    e) A_____of larks

BIRDS

1. Aristophanes.
2. Poe's Raven. "Nevermore."
3. The ostrich.
4. Percy Bysshe Shelley, "To a Skylark".
5. Gossamer is derived from "goose summer," that time of year, corresponding to Indian summer, when the goose is in season and a fine film of cobwebs is often seen floating in the air or caught on bushes or grass.
6. The shrike, or butcherbird.
7. The albatross, which has a wing span of over ten feet, can soar for hours without beating its wings. "The Rime of the Ancient Mariner", by Samuel Taylor Coleridge.

   'God save thee ancient Mariner!
   From fiends, that plague thee thus!—
   Why look'st thou so?—With my cross bow
   I shot the Albatross.

8. From its habit of defecating when flushed.
9. Because they are the property of the sovereign, and of two of the companies of the City of London, the Dyers and the Vintners.
10. a) bevy
    b) muster
    c) charm
    d) murmuration
    e) exaltation

BLACK HISTORY

1. Where is Zimbabwe located?
2. Why is Harriet Tubman remembered?
3. With which institution was the great agricultural chemist George Washington Carver associated for most of his life?
4. Whose autobiography was *Up from Slavery*?
5. For what is Matthew Henson noted?
6. Who called for complete black separatism, urged a "back to Africa" movement, and was the most influential black leader in the 1920s?
7. W. E. B. Du Bois was the co-founder of the National Negro Committee, which became what?
8. How did Jesse Owens upset Hitler's "Aryan" theories in 1936?
9. What was the Supreme Court decision in the 1954 case of *Brown* v. *Board of Education of Topeka, Kansas*?
10. Who were awarded Nobel Peace Prizes in 1950 and 1964?

BLACK HISTORY

1. It is the ruins of a famous city in Rhodesia, constructed by an early African people. Should black rule prevail in Rhodesia, Zimbabwe will probably be the new name of the country.

2. An escaped slave, she was a leading abolitionist and one of the most successful "conductors" on the Underground Railroad.

3. Tuskegee Institute in Alabama.

4. Booker T. Washington, a pioneer black educator who founded Tuskegee Institute.

5. Henson, who was a black man and Peary's servant, accompanied the explorer in his dash for the North Pole in 1909.

6. Marcus Garvey.

7. The National Association for the Advancement of Colored People (NAACP).

8. By his outstanding performance in the Olympic games in Berlin, where he equaled the world mark in the 100-meter dash, set world records in the 200-meter race and the broad jump, and was a member of the winning 400-meter relay team. Owens won four gold medals, and Hitler refused to shake his hand.

9. It declared that "separate educational facilities are inherently unequal" and ordered the nation's school systems desegregated.

10. Ralph Johnson Bunche, United Nations mediator, and Martin Luther King, Jr., clergyman and civil rights leader.

BRITISH ROYALTY AND PEERAGE

1. What is omitted from this list: Chester, Cornwall, Rothesay, Carrick, Renfrew, The Isles, Scotland?

2. Give in order of descending precedence, excluding royalty and clergy, the grades of the British peerage.

3. What is wrong with the legend about King Knut, otherwise known as Canute, taking his courtiers to the seashore to show he was so powerful that he could stop the tide from advancing?

4. What do the Dukedoms of Buccleuch, Grafton, Richmond, and St. Albans have in common?

5. Where in England is the sovereign not permitted to enter?

6. Who was the First Lord of the Admiralty who had an important group of islands named for him?

7. What was the original family name of the House of Windsor?

8. Many British military heroes who were created peers appended the locations of their most famous battles or campaigns to their names. Can you give the place names following the titles of Field Marshals Kitchener, Alexander, and Montgomery?

9. In 1978 what happened to British royalty for the first time since 1540?

10. Name the only peer wanted by Scotland Yard for murder. Should he be apprehended and convicted, what special privilege would he have if the death penalty were still in effect?

BRITISH ROYALTY AND PEERAGE

1. Wales. The list comprises the titles of Prince Charles, who is Earl of Chester, Duke of Cornwall and Rothesay, Earl of Carrick, Baron of Renfrew, Lord of the Isles, Great Steward of Scotland, and, of course, Prince of Wales.

2. Duke, marquess, earl, viscount, and baron.

3. Just the opposite is true. Tired of the flattery of his court, Canute showed them he was powerless to stem the tide.

4. They derive from extramarital affairs of Charles II with Lucy Walter; Barbara, Lady Castlemaine; Louise, Duchess of Portsmouth; and Nell Gwynn, respectively.

5. The House of Commons.

6. The fourth Earl of Sandwich, who had the Sandwich (now the Hawaiian) Islands named in his honor by Captain James Cook. It is probable that the Earl was responsible for the sandwich, which enabled him to eat without leaving the gaming table.

7. Wettin, which was the family name of Albert of Saxe-Coburg-Gotha, consort of Queen Victoria, was changed to Windsor by George V in 1917. Queen Elizabeth II, who married Philip Mountbatten, Duke of Edinburgh, decreed in 1952 that she and her children (except females who marry) shall be styled and known as the House and Family of Windsor.

8. Khartoum, Tunis, and Alamein.

9. A divorce, between Princess Margaret and Lord Snowdon. This was the first in the royal family since Henry VIII had his marriage to Anne of Cleves annulled. (George IV made an unsuccessful attempt, immediately after his accession to the throne in 1820, to divorce his long-estranged wife Caroline.)

10. The Earl of Lucan, for the murder of his children's nanny. He could choose to be hanged by a silken cord instead of a hempen rope.

BUILDINGS

1. A building owned by a triskaidekaphobiac would probably lack what?

2. Why might the Roman emperor Nero be considered to have made the word *palace* a common noun?

3. What is a hogan?

4. What color was the White House when it was built?

5. Where is the largest residential complex for an individual in the world?

6. Who designed the first geodesic dome?

7. Do you know the name of the most famous "temporary" structure in the world?

8. What was Versailles before it became a palace?

9. Of what famous building in England was this observation made: "It is as though St. Paul's had gone down to the sea and pupped"?

10. Why were *lupanar*s popular in ancient Rome, and how did the term originate?

BUILDINGS

1. A thirteenth floor, which would appear as the fourteenth. The long word means an abnormal fear of the number 13.
2. Because his residence was called the *palatium*, which meant literally "within the palisades." This word entered English as "paleys" and later became "palace."
3. It is an earth-covered Navaho dwelling.
4. The light gray of the Virginia freestone of which it was constructed. It was painted white after being set fire to in 1814 by British troops. Until the structure was rebuilt by Truman, one could see on damp days the scorch marks from Admiral Cockburn's vandalism come out above the windows.
5. The Vatican, in Rome.
6. Buckminster Fuller, the American architect and engineer.
7. The Eiffel Tower, which was built as an attraction for the Paris exposition of 1889 and named for its designer.
8. A hunting lodge.
9. The Royal Pavilion, also known as "The Onion Patch"; at Brighton in England. John Nash designed it for the Prince Regent in an ornate Eastern style featuring minarets and onion-domes.
10. They were brothels. The name comes from the Latin *lupa*, "she-wolf."

BUSINESS AND FINANCE

1. What common piece of furniture lends its name to a bank?
2. How did the Wall Street terms of a bull, for an optimistic buyer, and a bear, for a pessimistic seller, come into being?
3. Why does the word *nepotism*, or the practice of favoring relatives with jobs, have an ecclesiastical origin?
4. What was the origin of the sign of three gold balls over pawnshops?
5. Can you describe the South Sea Bubble?
6. The term *A-1* for first-rate was originally used in what type of business?
7. Who scored a great financial success as a result of the Battle of Waterloo?
8. A salary was originally an allowance given to Roman soldiers to buy what?
9. Securities, generally thought of as stocks and bonds, should, by derivation, be carefree. Why?
10. Special Drawing Rights (SDRs) are a type of international monetary reserve established by which agency:

BUSINESS AND FINANCE

1. A bench, where the earliest money-changers conducted their business. The Old Italian word for bench is *banca*, from which we get the modern word "bank."

2. From the fighting characteristics of these beasts. When a bull attacks, he lifts you up on his horns. When a bear attacks, he claws you down.

3. Nepotism derives from the practice of the early Popes, who often conferred special favors and ecclesiastical offices upon their "nephews" (Latin *nepotes*).

4. They are on the coat of arms of the Medici, early bankers.

5. A popular name in England for speculation in the South Sea Company, which in the early part of the eighteenth century had a monopoly of British trade with the islands of the South Seas and South America. It failed disastrously in 1720.

6. In the insurance business, particularly at Lloyd's of London, where the condition of a ship was so designated, the letters standing for its hull and the numbers for its equipment. (Lloyd's is named for Lloyd's Coffee House, in London, where marine underwriters used to meet.)

7. Nathan Rothschild, who was the first to receive the news, by carrier pigeon.

8. Salt.

9. Such investments are named from the Latin words *se* and *cura*, which are literally translated "free from care."

10. The International Monetary Fund, a specialized agency of the United Nations.

CAPITALS

1. Name three capitals that are planned cities.
2. Of which state is Tallinn the largest city and capital?
3. What and where is the Potala?
4. Where did Karl Marx do most of the research for his monumental *Das Kapital*?
5. Which world capital was once known variously as Edo, Yedo or Yeddo?
6. Near which capital are the ruins of ancient Carthage located?
7. Can you name a modern poet who eschewed capitals and who was, according to a publisher's note, "the terror of typesetters, an enigma to book reviewers, and the special target of all the world's literary philistines"?
8. Which is the only street in London where one drives on the right?
9. Give the meaning of the word Acropolis as in Athens.
10. Who beautified Washington, D.C., by planting poplars along Pennsylvania Avenue?

CAPITALS

1. Washington, D.C.; Canberra, in Australia; and Brasilia, Brazil.
2. Estonia, now a republic of the U.S.S.R.
3. It is the gigantic palace of the Dalai Lama located in Lhasa, the capital of Tibet.
4. In the reading room of the British Museum in London.
5. Tokyo, Japan.
6. Tunis, Tunisia.
7. e. e. cummings.
8. Savoy Court, off the Strand, leading to the Savoy Theatre and Savoy Hotel.
9. Highest town, from the Greek *akros*, topmost, and *polis*, city.
10. Thomas Jefferson.

CARTOONS AND COMIC STRIPS

1. In eighteenth-century England cartoons became an integral part of journalism largely through the works of which two artists?
2. What was the first comic strip to appear?
3. Who is regarded as the first American cartoonist?
4. Whose "swift singing sword" has fought Huns, Vikings, elephants, and gorillas?
5. Who drew the *New Yorker* cartoon of a large dog with mournful mien and the caption "He's been like this ever since Munich"?
6. What crime strip included such grotesque villains as The Brow, B-B Eyes, The Blank, Itchy, The Rodent, Pruneface, The Midget, Flyface, Flattop, The Mole, Measles, and Mumbles?
7. Who is the undisputed master of the macabre? Which television series was based on his work?
8. Which is the most widely syndicated comic strip?
9. Which caricaturist with a highly distinctive style incorporates the name of his daughter, Nina, a number of times in each of his line drawings?
10. Al Capp, in "Li'l Abner", probably assembled the most bizarre cast of characters to be found in the comic strip field. Can you recall the names of at least five of the denizens of Dogpatch?

CARTOONS AND COMIC STRIPS

1. Hogarth and Rowlandson.
2. "The Yellow Kid," who wore a bright yellow garment. This was drawn by R. F. Outcault and was first published in 1895 in the New York *World*, a Pulitzer paper. The use of yellow both here and later in the strips of the rival Hearst *Morning Journal* gave rise to the term "yellow journalism," referring to the sensational press of the time.
3. Benjamin Franklin, for his drawing of a snake severed in as many parts as there were colonies, and subtitled "Unite or Die." Published in the Philadelphia *Gazette* in 1754, it was instrumental in urging the colonies to unite.
4. Prince Valiant.
5. James Thurber.
6. "Dick Tracy," originated by Chester Gould in 1931, at a time when gangsterism during the Prohibition Era was rampant throughout the land.
7. Charles Addams. *The Addams Family*.
8. "Blondie," started by Chic Young in 1930, appears in over 1,600 papers in fifty countries.
9. Al Hirschfeld. The number of "ninas" in each drawing is shown to the right of the artist's signature.
10. Senator Jack S. Phogbound, Adam Lazonga, Evil-Eye Fleagle, Hairless Joe, Sir Cecil Cesspool, General Bullmoose, Joe Btfsplk, Marryin' Sam, Lonesome Polecat, Henry Cabbage Cod, J. Roaringham Fatback, and on the distaff side, Tobacco Rhoda, Stupefyin' Jones, Moonbeam McSwine, and Appasionata von Climax.

CATS AND DOGS

1. What is unique about Manx cats, and where did the breed originate?
2. Who was Cerberus?
3. Who described the archcriminal cat in these terms?

   > Macavity's a Mystery Cat; he's called the Hidden Paw—
   > For he's the master criminal who can defy the Law.
   > He's the bafflement of Scotland Yard, the Flying Squad's despair:
   > For when they reach the scene of crime—*Macavity's not there*!

4. Who were the respective owners of Fala, Flush, and Toto?
5. Can you give the origin of the phrase "not enough room to swing a cat"?
6. According to the U.S. Public Health Service, what are the three breeds of dog that bite the least? The most?
7. What was the name of the fictional cat who suddenly showed a surprising ability to understand and speak the English language, and then proceeded to thoroughly unnerve a proper English houseparty by commenting acidly on the activities and characters of the various houseguests?
8. Weimaraner dogs were first bred in Germany for hunting stags in which peculiar fashion?
9. What are seal points and blue points?
10. What have mad dogs and Englishmen in common, according to whom?

CATS AND DOGS

1. Manx cats, which are practically tailless, came from the Isle of Man.

2. In ancient mythology Cerberus was the three-headed dog who guarded the gates of Hades.

3. T. S. Eliot, in *Old Possum's Book of Practical Cats*.

4. Franklin Delano Roosevelt, Elizabeth Barrett Browning, and Dorothy, in *The Wonderful Wizard of Oz*.

5. This is a relic of the age of sail, when sailors were punished by means of a nine-thonged whip, called a "cat-o'-nine-tails," which left welts like the scratches of a huge cat. Since there was "not enough room to swing a cat" belowdecks, the punishment was administered topside.

6. Golden retriever, Labrador retriever, and Shetland sheepdog. German police dog, chow, and poodle.

7. Tobermory, in the short story of the same name by Saki (H. H. Munro).

8. They were trained to leap at a stag's genitals and rip them off.

9. Types of Siamese cats. Seal points have a pale fawn coat, while blue points have a gray one. Both types have darker ears, face, tail, and feet.

10. As Noël Coward said, "Mad dogs and Englishmen go out in the midday sun."

CHARACTERS IN LITERATURE

1. Who was "willin' "?
2. Natty Bumppo is the hero of which series of novels by whom?
3. Name the author of *Six Characters in Search of an Author*.
4. A picnic lunch of "coldtonguecoldhamcoldbeefpickledgherkins-saladfrenchrollscresssandwichespottedmeatgingerbeerle-monadesodawater" was shared by whom?
5. Which writer named his hero after a well-known authority on the birds of the West Indies?
6. Who was the bride of Angel Clare?
7. Why did a certain character sport a price tag bearing the legend: "In this style 10/6"?
8. In which novel is a leading character an American newspaper correspondent who was emasculated?
9. Who was "demned elusive"?
10. Where might you have found these colorful gentlemen: Harry the Horse, Franky Ferocious, Spanish John, Joey Uptown, Rope McGonnigle, Dancing Dan, Izzy Cheesecake, and Benny South Street?

CHARACTERS IN LITERATURE

1. Barkis, in Charles Dickens' *David Copperfield*, in which he sent a message to Clara Peggotty that "Barkis is willin'."
2. *Leatherstocking Tales*, by James Fenimore Cooper. The title is derived from the nickname of the hero, so called because of his long deerskin stockings.
3. Luigi Pirandello.
4. The Water Rat and the Mole, in Kenneth Grahame's *The Wind in the Willows*.
5. Ian Fleming, in his James Bond stories.
6. Tess Durbeyfield, in *Tess of the D'Urbervilles*, by Thomas Hardy.
7. Because he was the Mad Hatter in Lewis Carroll's *Alice in Wonderland*. The price of the hat was ten shillings sixpence.
8. *The Sun Also Rises*, Ernest Hemingway's first novel. The character was Jake Barnes.
9. The Scarlet Pimpernel, otherwise known as Sir Peter Blakeney, in a series of adventures about the French Revolution by Baroness Orczy (Mrs. Montague Barstow).

   We seek him here, we seek him there,
   Those Frenchies seek him everywhere.
   Is he in heaven?—Is he in hell?.
   That demned, elusive Pimpernel?

10. Most probably in Mindy's, Damon Runyon's name for Lindy's Restaurant, a famous former Broadway landmark.

CHILDREN'S LITERATURE

1. Name the superb literary stylist who wrote *Stuart Little, Charlotte's Web*, and *The Trumpet of the Swan*.
2. Name the character whose first words every morning were "What's for breakfast?"
3. In which novel did the ship *Hispaniola* play a large part?
4. Can you name the author of the Oz books?
5. What is the name of the reader on which many children of the nineteenth century were brought up?
6. Who was Peter Pan's fairy? What was the name of the land where the children encountered mermaids, Redskins, and pirates?
7. Who wrote *Toad of Toad Hall*?
8. Which novel has been called the "epic of American boyhood"?
9. For what is Sir John Tenniel most remembered?
10. What delightful fable was written by Antoine de Saint Exupéry?

CHILDREN'S LITERATURE

1. E. B. White
2. Winnie the Pooh.
3. *Treasure Island*, by Robert Louis Stevenson.
4. L. Frank Baum.
5. McGuffey's.
6. Tinker Bell. Neverland (not Never-Never Land).
7. A. A. Milne. The play is based on Kenneth Grahame's book *The Wind in the Willows*.
8. *Huckleberry Finn*.
9. The illustrations in *Alice's Adventures in Wonderland* and *Through the Looking-Glass*.
10. *The Little Prince*.

CHRISTMAS

1. Of which name is Santa Claus a contraction?
2. Who first described Santa Claus as a jolly fellow with a Dutch pipe, skimming over rooftops and dropping presents down chimneys?
3. What is the title of Clement Moore's famous poem about Christmas? How many times is Santa Claus mentioned in it?
4. Name Santa's "eight tiny reindeer" in the poem.
5. Which artist depicted Santa Claus as he is imagined today?
6. Is "Xmas" a proper abbreviation for Christmas?
7. In Charles Dickens' *A Christmas Carol*, what was the full name of Ebenezer Scrooge's late partner?
8. Can you correctly punctuate this traditional Yuletide greeting: "God rest you merry gentlemen".
9. Who was St. Nicholas?
10. In which work do the following lines concerning the Christmas season appear?

> It faded on the crowing of the cock.
> Some say that ever 'gainst that season comes
> Wherein our Savior's birth is celebrated,
> This bird of dawning singeth all night long,
> And then, they say, no spirit dare stir abroad,
> The nights are wholesome, then no planets strike,
> No fairy takes, nor witch hath power to charm:
> So hallowed and so gracious is that time.

CHRISTMAS

1. The Dutch *Sint Nikolaas* (Saint Nicholas). In the Netherlands and elsewhere the feast of St. Nicholas is celebrated on December 6, which is a children's holiday, when gifts are presented to them.

2. Washington Irving, using the pseudonym of Diedrich Knickerbocker, in *A History of New York*.

3. "A Visit From St. Nicholas", which begins " 'Twas the night before Christmas." Santa Claus is not mentioned at all, but St. Nicholas is.

4. Now, Dasher! now Dancer! now Prancer and Vixen!
On, Comet! on Cupid! on Donder and Blitzen!

5. The cartoonist Thomas Nast, in 1863.

6. Yes, it goes back to Old English. (The Greek word for "Christ" begins with the letter *chi*, or *x*.)

7. Jacob Marley.

8. "God rest you merry, gentlemen". The phrase "rest you merry" goes back to the fifteenth century.

9. A fourth century bishop of Myra, in Asia Minor. He is the patron saint of children and sailors, of Sicily, Greece, and Russia.

10. In the opening scene of Shakespeare's *Hamlet* when Marcellus, an officer of the guard, explains to Horatio the reason for the disappearance of the ghost of Hamlet's father, the dead King of Denmark.

CITIES AND TOWNS

1. Where would you find the Spanish Steps?
2. Give two former names of the city now known as Leningrad.
3. In which well-known play does the stage manager play an important role?
4. Which small city lends its name to an accent, a car, a cloth, a color, a dictionary, a Group, a marmalade, a Movement, and shoes?
5. Who was the author of the atheistic and despairing poem "The City of Dreadful Night"?
6. The name of which city is used as a verb meaning "to kidnap a person for compulsory service aboard a ship, especially after rendering him insensible"?
7. Which well-known magazine, according to its prospectus, was not written for the little old lady from Dubuque?
8. What was the name of the fabulous "City of Gold" which the early Spanish explorers sought in South America?
9. With which fictional city do you associate Babbitt in Sinclair Lewis' novel?
10. What do the following have in common: Atlanta, Bangor, Cleveland, Dayton, Hartford, Jacksonville, Newark, New Haven, Norfolk, Philadelphia, Phoenix, Stanford, and Urbana?

CITIES AND TOWNS

1. Rome, Italy.
2. St. Petersburg and Petrograd.
3. *Our Town*, by Thornton Wilder.
4. Oxford, England.
5. James Thomson.
6. Shanghai. This was fairly common practice in the China trade, especially on ships sailing between San Francisco and Shanghai.
7. The *New Yorker*.
8. El Dorado.
9. Zenith, a midwestern boom city.
10. They are all towns in New York State.

CLOTHES

1. What British peerage gave its title to a sofa, an overcoat, and a cigarette?
2. What uniform, still in use, did Michelangelo design?
3. The most popular clothes in the Western World are known as jeans, denims, and levis. Do you know the origins of these words?
4. In the world of fashion, who is Arnold Isaacs?
5. What were Cinderella's slippers made of?
6. Who described whom as "The glass of fashion and the mould of form"?
7. Where would you expect to find an aglet?
8. How did suede, or leather with a soft napped surface, come into the English language?
9. What is the only piece of headgear to be named after a poem?
10. Who originated the fashion of leaving the lower button of a vest or waistcoat unbuttoned?

CLOTHES

1. The Chesterfield family.
2. That worn by the Swiss Guard at the Vatican.
3. Jeans and denims are anglicized versions of two cities where the cloth was first made, Genoa in Italy and Nîmes in southern France, respectively. Levis owe their name to Levi Strauss, who, during the Gold Rush days in California, brought the coarse twilled material west with him to make tents and wagon covers for the miners. On finding they needed new pants more than tents, he adapted his cloth to this purpose. The company bearing his name still exists.
4. The couturier Arnold Scaasi, who reversed the spelling of his real last name.
5. Most likely of fur and not glass. It is believed that when Charles Perrault wrote down the Cinderella story in 1697, he mistook the old French word *vair*, meaning "ermine," for *verre*, which means "glass."
6. Ophelia, speaking of Hamlet, in Act III, Scene 1 of Shakespeare's play.
7. At the end of your shoelace. An aglet is the metal sheath attached to the end of a lace to facilitate its passing through the eyelet holes. It derives from the diminutive of the Latin *acus*, "needle."
8. From Sweden, which first exported this leather in the form of gloves. (French *gants de suède*, gloves of Sweden).
9. The tam-o'-shanter, from Robert Burns's "Tam o'Shanter".
10. King Edward VII, either inadvertently or because of his expanding girth.

CLUBS AND SOCIETIES

1. Who described a club as "an assembly of good fellows, meeting under certain conditions"?
2. The Society of the Cincinnati originally comprised whom?
3. What was "The Red-headed League"?
4. Can you name the chairman and the founding members of the Pickwick Club?
5. What has been called the "most exclusive club in the world"?
6. George Bernard Shaw's name is associated with which society, founded in 1883?
7. Of which club was Wodehouse's Bertie Wooster appropriately a member?
8. What was the Hell-Fire Club?
9. How many members are there in the Club of Rome, which was founded in 1968, and what are the objectives of the Club?
10. Who is reputed to have said, "I wouldn't join any club that would have me as a member."?

CLUBS AND SOCIETIES

1. Samuel Johnson, in his *Dictionary*. Dr. Johnson described Boswell as a "very clubable man."

2. The officers of the disbanding Continental army in 1783 and also Rochambeau's officers. (There is a French chapter as well.) Washington and Hamilton were its first presidents. It still exists as an organization of descendants of the founders, based on primogeniture.

3. The title of one of A. Conan Doyle's Sherlock Holmes stories, in which the League was a ploy to insure a successful bank robbery.

4. Mr. Samuel Pickwick and the Messrs. Tracy Tupman, Augustus Snodgrass, and Nathaniel Winkle. The adventures and misadventures of the members of this club formed the basis of Dickens' novel *The Pickwick Papers*.

5. The United States Senate.

6. The Fabian Society, which was formed to promote the gradual spread of socialism. It was named after the Roman general, Quintus Fabius Maximus Verrucosus, called *Cunctator* (Latin, delayer), who defeated Hannibal by harassment and by avoiding direct confrontation.

7. The Drones.

8. A notorious eighteenth-century coterie, devoted to conviviality and debauchery, which included naked masked women, weird religious rites, and drinking bouts. Among its members were Sir Francis Dashwood, John Wilkes, Charles Churchill, and the Earl of Sandwich. Benjamin Franklin was often a guest. The club first met in a ruined abbey and then in a series of immense caves on the Dashwood estate. These are now open to the public.

9. Membership is limited to one hundred and comprises humanists, scientists, educators, civil servants, and managers from more than thirty countries. Its objectives are to probe the nature of world problems and to stimulate political action.

10. Groucho Marx.

COLORS

1. In the context of the above, what do you suppose Roy G Biv means?
2. How did the phrase "red light district" originate?
3. What are the ingredients of the drink known as Black Velvet?
4. Literature's Hester Prynne was condemned to wear what for life?
5. What is patently redundant about the acronym WASP, meaning "White Anglo-Saxon Protestant"?
6. How did khaki originate as a shade for military uniforms?
7. What is the name of the "rose-red city, half as old as time," and in which country is it located?
8. In which war did the Order of the Purple Heart medal originate?
9. The subject of the popular song "The Object of My Affection" can do what?
10. When was the Mauve Decade?

COLORS

1. The letters represent the range of colors in the spectrum: red, orange, yellow, green, blue, indigo, violet.
2. From the red lamps the railroad men left outside the doors when they visited the brothels.
3. Champagne and stout.
4. A scarlet letter *A*, for adulteress. The novel, *The Scarlet Letter* established Nathanial Hawthorne's fame.
5. Have you ever heard of a black Anglo-Saxon?
6. The word "khaki" comes from the Persian *khak*, meaning "dust" or "earth." It was adopted by the British during the wars against the Sikhs in the mid-nineteenth century to replace the regulation red uniforms, which made too inviting a target.
7. Petra, in Jordan. The quotation is from the Newdigate Prize Poem, "Petra", by John William Burgon.
8. The American Revolution. The Order was established by George Washington in 1782, and the medal bears his likeness on one side. Originally intended to honor distinguished military service, it is now given to servicemen wounded in the line of duty.
9. "Change my complexion from white to rosy red."
10. The decade of the 1890s, which was called *La Belle Époque* in France. The name was used in the popular history of the era, *The Mauve Decade*, by Thomas Beer, who made a title-page bow to the painter James A. McNeill Whistler. ("Mauve?" asked Whistler. "Mauve is just pink trying to be purple.")

COMMUNICATION

1. When Samuel F. B. Morse in 1844 demonstrated to Congress the practicality of the electric telegraph, what famous message did he transmit from Washington to Baltimore?
2. Explain the difference between a post card and a postal card.
3. In Leigh Hunt's poem "Abou Ben Adhem," what message did Ben Adhem give to an angel writing in a book of gold "the names of those who love the Lord"?
4. What famous three-word alliterative phrase was born in one of Caesar's triumphal processions following a great victory? In what present-day country did this battle occur?
5. Which two letters are missing from the dials or push-buttons of telephones in the United States?
6. Does the international distress signal SOS mean "Save Our Ship," "Save Our Souls," or "Stop Other Signals"?
7. To what did the Ems dispatch lead?
8. Mayday, the international radio-telephone signal for aircraft and ships in distress, is the phonetic rendering of what phrase?
9. "Mr. Watson, come here. I want you," were the first words spoken into what?
10. Can you describe the "Ultra Secret" of World War II?

COMMUNICATION

1. "What hath God wrought!" (Numbers 23:23)
2. A postcard you buy and must stamp yourself; a postal card is sold by the post office with a stamp already affixed.
3. "Write me as one who loves his fellow men."

    The angel wrote and vanished. The next night
    it came again, with a great wakening light,
    And showed the names whom love of God had blessed,
    And lo! Ben Adhem's name led all the rest.
4. "Veni, vidi, vici" (I came, I saw, I conquered). In 47 B.C. Caesar defeated Pharnaces, King of Pontus, at Zela, which was located in northeast Asia Minor, now Turkey.
5. Q and Z.
6. None of them. It is simply an easily remembered Morse Code signal of three dits, three dahs, and three dits. It was adopted by international agreement in 1912.
7. This dispatch, which Bismarck transmitted to the press from Ems, brought on the Franco-Prussian War in 1870.
8. The French *m'aidez*, taken from a French psalm, which says "Help me, Lord."
9. The prototype telephone. These were the words spoken by Alexander Graham Bell into his first telephone in 1876 to an assistant one room away.
10. The "Ultra Secret," described as the outstanding cryptanalysis coup of the war, was the breaking of the German code by the British, who obtained a precise copy of the complex coding machine known as Enigma. This enabled the Allies to intercept and read many German signals throughout the war.

COUNTRIES

1. Which is the smallest country in the world?
2. In which country would you find Timbuktu, and for what was it famous?
3. Who said, "Something is rotten in the state of Denmark"?
4. What constitutes the United Kingdom?
5. Which country was named after a circle on the earth?
6. Where is Mont Blanc, the second highest peak in Europe, located?
7. What were the former names of Benin, Sri Lanka, Tanzania, Zaire, and Zambia?
8. Is Iran a new name for Persia?
9. Which maritime country has the shortest coastline?
10. Which nation did not change the spelling of its name, but by official edict changed its pronunciation?

COUNTRIES

1. The smallest independent country in the world is the State of the Vatican City, with an area of 108.7 acres. It also has the smallest population and a zero birth rate.

2. Mali, in northwest Africa, near the head of the River Niger. Timbuktu, which was settled in 1087 by the Tuareg, was a center of trade in gold, and its fame spread as far as Europe.

3. Marcellus, in Shakespeare's *Hamlet*.

4. Great Britain (England, Scotland, and Wales), Northern Ireland, the Isle of Man, and the Channel Islands. The official name is United Kingdom of Great Britain and Northern Ireland.

5. The Republic of Ecuador, because it is crossed by a great circle on the earth, the equator, which in Spanish is *ecquador*.

6. In France, on the Italian border. In 1860, when Savoy was ceded to France by Italy, certain of the peaks in the Mont Blanc Massif became French.

7. Dahomey, Ceylon, Tanganyika, Belgian Congo, and Northern Rhodesia.

8. No, the country has been known to the natives as Iran for centuries; foreigners called it Persia because they traded with the ancient kingdom of Pars (now the province of Fars) in the southwest part of Iran and bordering the Persian Gulf. The name Iran, which is derived from the same Indo-European root as "Aryan," was officially adopted in 1935.

9. Monaco, with a coastline of about 3½ miles.

10. Kenya was formerly pronounced "Keen-ya" but now is "Ken-ya," to rhyme with the last name of its first leader Jomo Kenyatta.

CRIME AND PUNISHMENT

1 What is the origin of the term "hoosegow"?

2. What is a "paper-hanger"?

3. Early in nineteenth-century India a murderous religious sect flourished, whose members were known by the Sanskrit word *sthaga*. To what has this been anglicized?

4. In which section of London did Jack the Ripper operate?

5. Can you identify Javert?

6. Who invented the guillotine?

7. How did *Passer Domesticus murder Erithacus Rubecula*?

8. Which type of drug user is responsible for the word "assassin"?

9. How did Scotland Yard get its name?

10. Name the authors who created the following fictional detectives:

   a) Nero Wolfe
   b) Philip Marlowe
   c) C. Auguste Dupin
   d) Lord Peter Wimsey
   e) Charlie Chan
   f) Inspector Maigret
   g) Sam Spade
   h) Miss Marple
   i) Father Brown
   j) Ellery Queen

CRIME AND PUNISHMENT

1. From the Spanish word *juzgado* used in Mexico, meaning jail.
2. A passer of counterfeit money.
3. Thug.
4. Whitechapel, in London's noisome east end, where he gruesomely murdered at least five unfortunate drabs.
5. He appears in Victor Hugo's novel *Les Misérables* as a police officer in whom devotion to duty has crushed all human sentiment.
6. The guillotine was conceived of during the Middle Ages, but it was Dr. Joseph Ignace Guillotin who advocated its use throughout France as a method of quick and painless death.
7. "I" said the Sparrow. "With my bow and arrow. I killed Cock Robin." All the birds of the air fell a-sighing and a-sobbing when they heard of the death of poor Cock Robin.
8. A marijuana, or hashish, user. In the olden Arabic days these people were called *hashshashin*, or hashish-eaters, from which assassin is derived.
9. Because it stood on the site of a palace where the Scottish kings once lived when they visited England.
10. a) Rex Stout
    b) Raymond Chandler
    c) Edgar Allan Poe
    d) Dorothy Sayers
    e) Earl Derr Biggers
    f) Georges Simenon
    g) Dashiell Hammett
    h) Agatha Christie
    i) G. K. Chesterton
    j) Ellery Queen (Frederic Dannay and Manfred B. Lee)

DANCE

1. What was the kordax?

2. In the early Renaissance, court dances became popular with established step patterns and rules. Can you name three out of seven of these dances? What form of music was developed from these?

3. In the field of dance, what notable event occurred at the court of Catherine de' Medici, Queen of Henry II of France?

4. Which king, who was a ballet dancer from the age of 13, founded the Royal Ballet Company?

5. With which countries are these dances associated: czardas, fandango, mazurka, tarantella, and the jig?

6. In 1909, who took to Paris a Russian company which dominated the world of dance? Name three of the leading choreographers and dancers from this company.

7. How did the famous American dancer Isadora Duncan meet her death in 1927?

8. Name one of the leaders of the modern dance revolution whose earliest appearances were on the Keith-Orpheum vaudeville circuit.

9. Who specialized in dancing up and down stairs? Who made appearing to dance on the walls and ceiling famous?

10. In 1951, 1961, and 1968 which three choreographers won honorary Oscars for their work in films?

DANCE

1. It was an ancient Dionysian phallic dance performed in the nude.
2. Galliard, pavane, allemande, courante, saraband, gigue, and minuet. The sonata developed from these.
3. The first ballet which combined music, movement, and decoration was presented.
4. Louis XIV of France, in 1661.
5. Hungary, Spain, Poland, Italy, and Ireland.
6. Sergei Diaghilev. Michel Fokine, Léonide Massine, Vaslav Nijinsky, Anna Pavlova, and George Balanchine.
7. Her neck was broken when the long scarf she was wearing became entangled in a rear wheel of her car while she was motoring in Nice.
8. Martha Graham, who followed Isadora Duncan and Ruth St. Denis.
9. Bill "Bojangles" Robinson. Fred Astaire.
10. Gene Kelly, for *An American in Paris*; Jerome Robbins, for *West Side Story*; and Onna White, for *Oliver*.

DAYS AND DATES

1. In a speech before a session of the Joint Houses of Congress, President Franklin D. Roosevelt referred to "a date which will live in infamy." What was the date?
2. How many birthdays does Queen Elizabeth have each year?
3. Why is August 12 referred to as "the glorious twelfth" in England and Scotland?
4. Our names for the days of the week are derived from the Roman, Old Norse, and Anglo-Saxon. Without going into these ancient roots, can you tell for whom each day is named?
5. How did the ice cream sundae get its name?
6. In Shakespeare's *Julius Caesar* a soothsayer warns Caesar to "Beware the ides of March." To which day is he referring?
7. What does the *D* in D-Day stand for? In which war was the term first used?
8. When does Boxing Day fall in Great Britain, and how did the name begin?
9. What will be the first day of the twenty-first century?
10. When did we start to reckon time from a theoretical birthdate of Christ?

DAYS AND DATES

1. December 7, 1941, the date of the Japanese attack on Pearl Harbor.
2. Two. One is her actual birthday, in April, and the other is what is called her official birthday, on a Saturday in early June, which is celebrated by the colorful ceremony of the Trooping of the Colour.
3. The date marks the opening of the grouse-shooting season.
4. Monday, day of the moon; Tuesday, day of Tiw (a god of war); Wednesday, day of Woden (chief deity); Thursday, day of Thor (god of Thunder); Friday, day of Frigg (Woden's wife); Saturday, day of Saturn; Sunday, the day of the sun.
5. This concoction apparently first appeared in an ice cream parlor in Wisconsin, where it was served only on Sundays, hence the name. The "-ae" ending was undoubtedly added later to lend a touch of class to the dish.
6. March 15, according to the old Roman calendar.
7. Day, so the term literally means "Day-day." It was first used in World War I to designate the start of the Allied offensive at Saint-Mihiel.
8. It is the first *weekday*, not necessarily the first day, after Christmas and is observed as a holiday. On that day it is customary to present gifts, or boxes, to household employees and other service workers.
9. January 1, 2001. (This will become clear when you consider the fact that the first century ended on December 31, 100, which marked the passing of the first hundred years.)
10. Since the sixth century, when Dionysius Exiguus, a monk and chronologist, conceived the idea. Prior to that, time was based on the date of the founding of Rome by Romulus, which was traditionally set at 753 B.C. This system was called *ab urbe condita*, or AUC—that is, from the founding of the city.

DOWNSTAIRS

1. What were the names of the cook and the butler of the Bellamy household in the British television series "Upstairs, Downstairs," and who played these parts?
2. Name the nanny who had a perfectly rolled umbrella with a parrot handle.
3. On Olympus, what were the duties of Hebe and Ganymede?
4. In England, what is a "tweeny"?
5. Identify Jean Passepartout.
6. Who played the part of Prissy, Scarlett O'Hara's high-strung maid, in *Gone with the Wind*?
7. Who said, "The cook was a good cook, as cooks go; and as cooks go she went."
8. Describe the nurse of the Darling children in *Peter Pan*.
9. Can you name four works of fiction in English which showed that the valet or butler was invariably superior to his employer?
10. Who wrote, "They also serve who only stand and wait."?

DOWNSTAIRS

1. Mrs. Bridges and Mr. Hudson, played by Angela Baddeley and Gordon Jackson.
2. Mary Poppins.
3. They were cupbearers to the gods.
4. A maid who assists both the cook and the housemaid; otherwise known as a betweenmaid, hence the term "tweeny."
5. Phileas Fogg's French servant who accompanied him on his trip around the world in eighty days, as described in the Jules Verne novel. (*Passepartout* in French means go everywhere and also a master key.)
6. Butterfly McQueen.
7. Saki, in *Reginald*.
8. She was a Newfoundland dog called Nana.
9. *Right Ho! Jeeves* (and others), by P. G. Wodehouse; *Ruggles of Red Gap*, by H. L. Wilson; *My Man Godfrey*, by Eric Hatch; and *The Admirable Crichton*, by Sir James M. Barrie.
10. John Milton, in the sonnet "On His Blindness."

DRINK

1. In a "bourbon and branch," what is "branch"?
2. The initials D.O.M. appear on the label of every bottle of Benedictine. What do they mean?
3. For what should John Styth Pemberton, a pharmacist, be remembered?
4. Tabasco, which enhances a Bloody Mary, is named for what?
5. Which types of spirit are correctly spelled whisky?
6. Name the favorite drink of the Vikings, and its chief ingredient.
7. How did the expression "mind your p's and q's" possibly originate?
8. What was the old Gaelic word, meaning "water of Life," from which the word "whisky" is derived?
9. Who was the sage who observed the following?

   Candy
   is dandy
   But liquor
   Is quicker.

10. "Let's get out of these wet clothes and into a dry martini" was said by whom?

DRINK

1. Water, specifically "branch water," such as water from a stream, creek, or brook.
2. *Deo Optimo Maximo* (L.), to God, the Best, the Greatest: motto of the Benedictines.
3. He concocted the original Coca-Cola mixture in Atlanta in 1886.
4. Tabasco, a state in Mexico, the source of the peppers originally used in the sauce.
5. Only Scotch and Canadian. Irish, bourbon, and rye are spelled "whiskey."
6. Mead, a liquor, made from fermenting a mixture of honey and water.
7. From the custom in English pubs of listing the patrons' beer orders on a board marked p and q, for pints and quarts.
8. Usquaebach (one of several variants of the Gaelic). There is a brand of single malt Scotch sold under this name.
9. Ogden Nash, "Reflections on Ice-Breaking," from *Many Long Years Ago*.
10. Robert Benchley (*not* Dorothy Parker or Alexander Woollcott).

ENGLISH LITERATURE

1. Name the last and unfinished novel by Charles Dickens.
2. Shelley's poem "Adonais" is an elegy on the death of whom?
3. What are considered to be the first full-length detective novels in English, and who was the author?
4. Can you identify the famous poem which was written under the influence of opium?
5. Which novelist of Polish parentage wrote in English?
6. What is wrong about these lines from Keats's sonnet "On First Looking into Chapman's Homer"?

   "Or like stout Cortez when with eagle eyes
       He star'd at the Pacific—and all his men
   Look'd at each other with a wild surmise—
       Silent, upon a peak in Darien."

7. Who introduced Sherlock Holmes to Dr. Watson?
8. Which character "lards the lean earth as he walks along"?
9. What was significant about the discovery of the Isham Papers in Malahide Castle, Ireland, early in this century?
10. In which poem did a nineteenth-century writer foresee air transport, air warfare, and the United Nations?

ENGLISH LITERATURE

1. *The Mystery of Edwin Drood.*
2. John Keats.
3. *The Woman in White* and *The Moonstone*, by Wilkie Collins.
4. "Kubla Khan", by Samuel Taylor Coleridge.
5. Joseph Conrad.
6. Balboa was the first Spaniard to look out over the Pacific, not Cortez.
7. Young Stamford, whom Watson ran into at the Criterion Bar off Piccadilly Circus at a time when he was looking for lodgings. Stamford took Watson to St. Bartholomew's Hospital, where Holmes was working in a chemical laboratory. See the opening of "A Study in Scarlet."
8. Falstaff, in Shakespeare's *Henry IV*, Part I.
9. A great mass of James Boswell's manuscripts—letters, journals, and other papers—came to light. Lt. Col. Ralph T. Isham purchased these in 1927 and later sold them to Yale University.
10. "Locksley Hall", by Alfred, Lord Tennyson, as shown in the following lines:

> For I dipt into the future, far as human eye could see,
> Saw the Vision of the world, and all the wonder that would be;
> Saw the heavens fill with commerce, argosies of magic sails,
> Pilots of the purple twilight, dropping down with costly bales;
> Heard the heavens fill with shouting, and there rain'd a ghastly dew,
> From the nations' airy navies grappling in the central blue;
>
> . . . .
>
> Till the war-drum throbb'd no longer, and the battle-flags were furl'd
> In the Parliament of Man, the Federation of the world.

EUROPEAN HISTORY

1. What was the name of the last Saxon king of England, who was overthrown and killed in the same year he gained the throne?
2. Describe the Domesday Book.
3. For what exploit is Godfrey de Bouillon famous?
4. Who met on "The Field of Cloth of Gold"?
5. Who transferred the capital of Russia from Moscow to St. Petersburg early in the eighteenth century?
6. Which Italian family ruled Florence during Renaissance times?
7. Who crowned Napoleon at Nôtre Dame in 1804?
8. Charles Stewart Parnell is a hero to the people of what country?
9. What event triggered World War I?
10. Why was September 1, 1939, a significant date?

EUROPEAN HISTORY

1. King Harold, who was defeated by William the Conqueror in 1066 at the Battle of Hastings.
2. A statistical survey of the lands of England, made by King William I in 1086.
3. His leadership of the First Crusade, from 1096 to 1100.
4. Henry VIII of England met François I of France in 1520, on a field near Calais in company with the courts of both rulers. (The phrase "Cloth of Gold" refers not to a carpeting, but to the color of the tents. The meeting place is often erroneously referred to as "The Field of the Cloth of Gold.")
5. Peter the Great, so that Russia could have "a window to the West."
6. The Medici.
7. He crowned himself, although Pope Pius VII was present to perform that function.
8. Ireland. He was an Irish Member of Parliament who was active in the interests of Ireland.
9. The assassination of the Archduke Franz Ferdinand of Austria at Sarajevo, Bosnia, in June 1914.
10. It marked the beginning of World War II, when Germany invaded Poland without a declaration of war.

EXPLORATION

1. Who is reported to have said, "Along this track of pathless ocean I intend to steer."?
2. What was the first English possession outside Europe, and who established it?
3. Who was the first man to set foot on all the continents, excluding Antarctica?
4. Who discovered Florida, and why was it so named?
5. Of what nationality was the famous explorer John Cabot?
6. Who named the Pacific Ocean?
7. Sacajawea, an American Indian, accompanied which expedition as guide and the only woman in the party?
8. What was the name of Henry Hudson's ship?
9. Whose was the second party to reach the South Pole?
10. Who was the first to fly over the North Pole, and when was this flight made?

EXPLORATION

1. Christopher Columbus, the Admiral of the Ocean Sea, as Samuel Eliot Morrison titled his book about the great explorer.
2. Newfoundland, in Canada. Its discovery in 1583 by Sir Humphrey Gilbert, the elder half-brother of Sir Walter Raleigh, marked the beginning of the British Empire.
3. Captain James Cook.
4. Ponce de León, on Easter Sunday 1513. He named the land in honor of that day which in Spanish is *Pascua Florida*, or Flowery Easter.
5. Venetian. His real name was Giovanni Caboto.
6. Ferdinand Magellan, because of its peaceful appearance after he emerged from the Strait of Magellan.
7. The Lewis and Clark Expedition, which explored the territory of the Louisiana Purchase and the country beyond to the Pacific Ocean.
8. The *Half Moon*.
9. Captain Robert Scott, who failed in his race to the Pole with the Norwegian explorer, Roald Amundsen. Scott and his companions perished from the cold on the return trip to their base in January 1912.
10. Commander Richard E. Byrd, in the *Josephine Ford* on May 9, 1926. Amundsen, Ellsworth, and Nobile followed him three days later.

FAMILIAR MISQUOTATIONS

Can you complete these popular quotes correctly?

1. "All that_____is not gold."
2. "To_____the lily"
3. "_____ is the hobgoblin of little minds."
4. "A little_____is a dangerous thing."
5. "Alas! poor Yorick,_____"
6. "Imitation is the sincerest_____flattery."
7. "_____is a rose is a rose."
8. "Music has charms to soothe a_____"
9. "Water, water everywhere_____drop to drink"
10. "_____, my dear Watson."

FAMILIAR MISQUOTATIONS

1. glistens (Shakespeare, *The Merchant of Venice*)
2. paint (Shakespeare, *King John*)
3. A foolish consistency (Emerson, *Essays*—"Self-Reliance")
4. learning (Pope, *Essay on Criticism*)
5. I knew him, Horatio (Shakespeare, *Hamlet*)
6. of (Colton, *The Lacon*)
7. Rose (Gertrude Stein, "Sacred Emily")
8. savage breast (Congreve, *The Mourning Bride*)
9. nor any (Coleridge, *The Rime of the Ancient Mariner*)
10. If you answered "Elementary," you are mistaken; in none of the Conan Doyle stories does Sherlock Holmes ever utter this phrase. In "The Crooked Man," however, when Watson cries, "Excellent!", Holmes replies, "Elementary."

FEDERALESE AND ASSORTED GOBBLEDYGOOK

Federal Prose is that form of nonmetrical composition, apparently English, which can be invariably interpreted as meaning and/or not meaning more and/or less than, rather than what, it seems to mean.

Rule 1. Never say anything clearly that, with a little more effort, can be made practically unintelligible.

Rule 2. Do not hesitate to obfuscate.

Some of the following are deliberate examples of circumlocution. The others will be recognized as favorites of those in government, the groves of academe, particularly in the social sciences, and other recondite fields. How many can you put into correct, simple English?

1. Prior to, anterior to.
2. Precipitation entails negation of economy.
3. Viable.
4. The initiation of the termination.
5. Radiation enhancement weapon.
6. Solar bodies tend to exhibit, with respect to and from the viewpoint of their satellites, an apparent orientality of anabasis.
7. Dichotomy.
8. In every canine lifespan is manifested a period of optimum euphoria.
9. Don't initiate protective reaction prior to establishment of firm eyeball identification.
10. "It is not an avocation of a remunerative description," in the memorable words of Mr. Micawber in *David Copperfield*.

FEDERALESE AND ASSORTED GOBBLEDYGOOK

1. Before.
2. Haste makes waste.
3. Possible, practical, feasible.
4. The beginning of the end.
5. The pentagon term for the neutron bomb, which kills every living creature within its reach but leaves inanimate structures unharmed.
6. The sun rises in the east.
7. Split, division.
8. Every dog has his day.
9. Don't fire until you see the whites of their eyes.
10. "In other words, it does *not* pay." (Mr. Micawber was then "engaged in the sale of corn upon commission.")

FICTIONAL FAREWELLS

Name the character who uttered the following final words, which may or may not be dying words.

1. "Rosebud."
2. "O, I am slain!"
3. "For the love of God! Montresor!"
4. "Mother of Merry, is this the end of Rico?"
5. "I've had such a curious dream!"
6. "Thus with a kiss I die."
7. "Louis, I think this is the beginning of a beautiful friendship."
8. "What should I stay—"
9. "It is a far, far better thing that I do, then I have ever done; it is a far, far better rest that I go to, than I have ever known."
10. "Where am I? What am I doing? Why? God forgive me everything!"

FICTIONAL FAREWELLS

1. Charles Foster Kane (Orson Welles), in the film *Citizen Kane*. ("Rosebud" was the name on his boyhood sled.)
2. Polonius, in Shakespeare's *Hamlet*.
3. Fortunato, in Poe's *A Cask of Amontillado*.
4. Caesar Rico Bandello (Edward G. Robinson), in the film *Little Caesar*.
5. Alice, in *Alice in Wonderland*.
6. Romeo, in Shakespeare's *Romeo and Juliet*.
7. Rick Blaine (Humphrey Bogart), to Captain Louis Renault (Claude Rains) at the end of the film *Casablanca*.
8. Cleopatra, in Shakespeare's *Antony and Cleopatra*.
9. Sidney Carton, in *A Tale of Two Cities*, by Charles Dickens.
10. Anna, in Leo Tolstoy's *Anna Karenina*.

FIGHTING WORDS

Who said the following?

1. "Put your faith in God, but keep your powder dry."
2. "Surrender this fort . . . In the name of the Great Jehovah and the Continental Congress."
3. "I have not yet begun to fight."
4. "England expects every man will do his duty."
5. "Don't give up the ship!"
6. "We have met the enemy, and they are ours."
7. "The Guard dies, but never surrenders."
8. "Damn the torpedoes! Go ahead! Full speed!"
9. "You may fire when you are ready, Gridley."
10. "Nuts!"

FIGHTING WORDS

1. Oliver Cromwell, to his troops when they were crossing a river to attack the enemy.
2. Ethan Allen, the leader of the Green Mountain Boys, when he took Fort Ticonderoga in the early days of the American Revolution.
3. John Paul Jones, aboard the *Bonhomme Richard* in 1779.
4. Horatio, Viscount Nelson. This was Nelson's signal to his fleet before the Battle of Trafalgar in 1805.
5. Captain James Lawrence shouted this as he was carried, mortally wounded, from the deck of his ship, the *Chesapeake*, which had engaged a British frigate blockading Boston during the War of 1812. His brave words were in vain, however, for the *Chesapeake* struck her colors.
6. Oliver Hazard Perry in a message to General Harrison after defeating the British at the Battle of Lake Erie in 1813.
7. As the Battle of Waterloo was drawing to a close, the English sent a message to Napoleon's famous Imperial Guard asking them to surrender. The phrase was attributed to Count Cambronne, who denied saying it. Apparently it was dreamed up by a journalist two days later. It has been reported that what was really said was "Merde!" (Shit!)
8. David Glasgow Farragut, the outstanding naval commander in the Civil War, during the Battle of Mobile Bay in 1864. (The "torpedoes" referred to are not those we know today as they had not been invented yet; Farragut meant "mines." To be more precise, they were beer kegs filled with powder.)
9. Commodore George Dewey, to the captain of his flagship at the Battle of Manila Bay in 1898.
10. General Anthony McAuliffe, replying on December 23, 1944, to a German demand for the surrender of the 101st Airborne Division, which had been trapped for seven days at Bastogne during the Battle of the Bulge.

FIRE

1. In what guise did God first talk to Moses?
2. Who was the author of the novel *Pale Fire*?
3. At sea the appearance of St. Elmo's fire as fiery emanations from the tips of a ship's mast or spar is regarded as what?
4. On which island did the volcano of Mount Pelée erupt in 1902, with the loss of 40,000 lives?
5. Do you know the legend of how the great Chicago fire of 1871 was supposed to have started?
6. What causes most forest fires?
7. Who wrote *The Fire Next Time*, a series of essays on the feelings and attitudes of U.S. blacks?
8. Why do fireflies light up?
9. Hephaestos and Vulcan have what in common?
10. Can you name the Poet Laureate who wrote the following?

    Only stay quiet while the mind remembers
    The beauty of fire from the beauty of embers.

FIRE

1. As a bush that "burned with fire, and the bush was not consumed." (Exodus 1.8)
2. Vladimir Nabokov.
3. A portent of bad weather.
4. Martinique.
5. Mrs. O'Leary's cow kicked over a lantern. It later developed that a reporter made up the story to lend color to his article on the fire.
6. Lightning.
7. James Baldwin.
8. As a form of sexual attraction. It is thought that the intensity and frequency of the flashes serve to identify males and females to one another.
9. They are respectively the Greek and Roman gods of fire and metalworking.
10. John Masefield, "On Growing Old."

FLIGHT

1. How were the wings of a mythical ill-fated flier secured?
2. Where may the world's most famous winged statue be seen?
3. For what were the Montgolfier brothers famous?
4. Why is the date December 17, 1903, memorable in the annals of aviation?
5. Who was the top-ranking ace of World War I, and how many planes is he credited with shooting down?
6. What led to the court martial of General Billy Mitchell in 1925?
7. For what use was the tower of the Empire State Building originally intended?
8. Who gave this tribute to which force during World War II: "Never in the field of human conflict was so much owed by so many to so few."?
9. Can you identify the lady named as Enola Gay?
10. With the advent of supersonic flight, by what unit is the speed of supersonic aircraft measured? What does this unit mean?

FLIGHT

1. Icarus' wings were fastened with wax, which melted under the rays of the sun.
2. The "Nike" or "Winged Victory of Samothrace" may be seen in the Louvre Museum, Paris. Carved at the end of the fourth century B.C., it commemorated a naval victory.
3. They invented the first practical man-carrying balloon in France, in 1783.
4. That was the date when Orville and Wilbur Wright made the first controlled, sustained flights in a power-driven airplane near Kitty Hawk, North Carolina.
5. Manfred von Richthofen, nicknamed "the Red Baron" for the color of the planes he flew, had eighty allied aircraft to his credit when he was killed in action in 1918.
6. His sharp criticism of military leaders for their neglect of air power. World War II, which saw the adoption of many of his ideas, largely vindicated him. The exact charge against him at this courtmartial was insubordination.
7. For the mooring of dirigibles, a plan which never proved feasible.
8. Prime Minister Winston Churchill, in a tribute to the Royal Air Force, in the House of Commons, August 1940.
9. She was the mother of Colonel Paul Tibbets, Jr., who commanded the B-29, named for her, that dropped the first atomic bomb on Hiroshima in 1945 and led to the Japanese surrender.
10. By Mach number. Mach 1 equals the speed of sound at a given altitude (approximately 760 mph at sea level and about 650 mph above 35,000 feet). Mach 2 is twice as fast. This system was named for Dr. Ernst Mach, an Austrian physicist who had experimented with supersonics. Speeds between Mach 1 and Mach 5 are known as supersonic, and above Mach 5, hypersonic.

FOOD

1. How did the ubiquitous hot dog get its name?
2. What does the southern dish known as chitterlings or chitlins consist of?
3. What is the probable derivation of mayonnaise?
4. Can you identify the edible fruit whose name is derived from the Nahuatl word for "testicle"?
5. What is Bombay Duck, and when is it served?
6. Why is corned beef so named?
7. Which three ingredients are chiefly responsible for the distinctive flavor of Worcestershire sauce?
8. Why is chowder named after a pot?
9. What is a sweetbread?
10. What is the name of a type of French eating establishment that came into the French language in 1814, during the post-Napoleonic occupation of Paris by the victorious troops of Czar Alexander I?

FOOD

1. From a cartoon of a dachsund inside an elongated bun. This was drawn by the popular sports cartoonist T. A. Dorgan, who signed his work TAD, early in the century when the product was widely supposed to contain dog meat.
2. The small intestines of pigs.
3. It is believed that mayonnaise was named to commemorate the capture of the city of Mahón, capital of Minorca in the Balearic Islands, by the Duc de Richelieu in 1756.
4. The avocado, from the Nahuatl *ahuacatl* (In Spanish, *aguacate*).
5. It is a dried fish which is served as an accompaniment to curries.
6. Corned beef is beef preserved in salt, which at one time was in the form of pellets called corns.
7. Anchovies, soy, and tamarinds.
8. In Brittany it was the custom for each fisherman to throw his catch into a community pot, or *chaudière*. The fame of this dish was such that it spread to Newfoundland and then to the east coast of the United States. The name of the pot was applied to its contents and restyled "chowder."
9. The thymus gland of an animal.
10. Bistro, from *bystra*, the Russian word for "quickly." It seems that certain sections of Paris were out of bounds to the Russians, and when the soldiers, disobeying the order, went into a tavern, they demanded fast service so that the patrols would not catch them.

FOREIGN TERMS AND PHRASES

Give the English equivalent of the following:

1. *Vis-à-vis* (Fr.)
2. *Quid pro quo* (L.)
3. *Der Mensch ist was er isst* (Ger.)
4. *Così von tutti* (It.)
5. *Amour-propre* (Fr.)
6. *Salaam aleikum* (Ar.)
7. *Dies Irae* (L.)
8. *Liebe kann viel, Geld kann alles* (Ger.)
9. *Soi-disant* (Fr.)
10. *Honi soit qui mal y pense* (Fr.)

FOREIGN TERMS AND PHRASES

1. Face to face; opposite.
2. Something in return; a substitute.
3. Man is what he eats.
4. Thus do they all; that is the way of the world.
5. Self-esteem; vanity.
6. Peace be with you: Moslem salutation.
7. Day of wrath; hence, Day of Judgment: a Latin hymn sung at solemn requiems.
8. Love is mighty, but money is almighty.
9. Self-styled; pretended, would-be.
10. Shame on him who thinks evil of it: the motto of England's Most Noble Order of the Garter, the highest the Monarch can bestow. It comprises twenty-six knights only, including the Sovereign.

GAMES

1. What is the world's largest-selling game?
2. Who invented contract bridge?
3. In gambling casinos, which common object is generally missing?
4. Who was the compulsive gambler who wrote a novel titled *The Gambler*?
5. "Tables" and "tric-trac" were the former names for what popular game?
6. The numbers on opposite sides of a die add up to what?
7. What game is played with pegs? With tiles?
8. Can you name the six pieces used in chess?
9. *The Art of Winning Games Without Actually Cheating* is the subtitle of what classic work on games?
10. What does the poker term "dead man's hand" mean, and how did it originate?

GAMES

1. "Monopoly." More than 80 million "Monopoly" games have been sold since 1935 when Parker Brothers bought it from its inventor, Charles B. Darrow.
2. Harold S. Vanderbilt, while on a cruise through the Caribbean in 1925. It superseded auction bridge.
3. There are no clocks to be seen.
4. Fyodor Dostoyevsky.
5. Backgammon.
6. Seven.
7. Cribbage. Mah-Jongg.
8. King, queen, rook (or castle), bishop, knight, and pawn.
9. *Gamesmanship*, by Stephen Potter.
10. It is a pair of aces and a pair of eights together ("aces over eights"). This was the hand that "Wild Bill" Hickok was holding when he was shot from behind and killed in Deadwood, Dakota Territory, in 1876.

A GARDEN OF CURIOSITIES

1. The Greek goddess of the rainbow is responsible for the name of what flower of varied and striking colors?
2. To what flower, with its sunburst center and radiant petals, was Chaucer referring when he wrote "the eye of day"?
3. Why is an anemone sometimes called a windflower?
4. What type of clover was used by St. Patrick as his symbol?
5. Why does the dainty pansy wear such a "thoughtful" mien?
6. Can you describe a desert rose?
7. For whom was the poinsettia named, and why is it considered an appropriate Christmas plant?
8. Where was the scene of the agony of Jesus?
9. Where did Monet paint his famous water lilies?
10. The name of what flower is derived from the Greek word for testicle, which it resembles because of its double roots?

A GARDEN OF CURIOSITIES

1. Iris.
2. The daisy.
3. Because its name derives from *anemos*, the Greek word for wind.
4. The shamrock, which was supposedly used by St. Patrick to illustrate the Trinity because of its three leaves.
5. Because its original name was *pensée*, French for "thought," which developed into "pansy."
6. It is not a flower at all but a rock, consisting of grains of sand fused together, the surface of which has been eroded by the elements so that it resembles a rose. Desert roses are commonly found in the Sahara.
7. Joel Roberts Poinsett, of Charleston, South Carolina, who after a mission to Mexico brought the plant with the large flaming leaves back to the United States. Poinsettias are favored at Christmas because the leaves generally stay red until Easter.
8. The Garden of Gethsemane, outside Jerusalem.
9. In his garden at Giverny, France. It is being restored by the generosity of the Lila Acheson Wallace Foundation.
10. Orchid, from *orchis*, testicle.

GOLF AND TENNIS

1. What is the full name of the international shrine of Golf?
2. Which is more commonly played in this country, lawn tennis or court tennis?
3. What royal association may be attached to the word "caddie"?
4. Why is the name of Major Walter C. Wingfield remembered?
5. Which three countries compete in the amateur biennial Walker Cup golf competition?
6. In which of Shakespeare's plays do you find tennis balls?
7. Can you explain how Joyce Wethered managed in 1927 to get two birdies in one hole?
8. Give one of the many derivations for the words "tennis," "set," and "love."
9. In 1930 Bobby Jones became the first person to achieve a Grand Slam—that is, winning the U.S. Amateur and Open, and the British Amateur and Open championships. For a Grand Slam today a player must win which four tournaments? Who was the first golfer to do this?
10. Who was the first man to win three consecutive Wimbledon championships since Fred Perry's string in the thirties?

CARL A. RUDISILL LIBRARY
LENOIR-RHYNE COLLEGE

GOLF AND TENNIS

1. The Royal and Ancient Golf Club of St. Andrews, Scotland, founded in 1754.

2. Lawn tennis. Court tennis, royal or real tennis (it was formerly a favorite of royalty), is played on a complex indoor court and dates back to medieval France, where it probably originated within the castle walls. It is the forerunner of most modern racquet games.

3. When Mary, Queen of Scots, returned to Scotland in 1561, she brought both her French court and a passion for golf. To retrieve her golf balls she used her young pages, who were called by the French word *cadet*. This later evolved into caddie.

4. He invented lawn tennis in 1873. It came to the United States in 1874, where it was first called *sphairistike*, meaning "ball play" in Greek.

5. Great Britain and Ireland versus the United States.

6. *Henry V.*

7. Her drive struck a swallow.

8. "Tennis" may be derived from the French *tenez*, an interjection approximating "Look here!" "Set" probably comes from *sept*, dating from the days when it took seven, not six, games to make a set. For "love" we have the French for the egg, *l'oeuf*, signifying zero.

9. The U.S. Open, the Masters, the PGA, and the British Open. No golfer has ever done it.

10. Bjorn Borg, in 1978.

GOVERNMENT

1. What are the first ten amendments to the Constitution frequently called?
2. Which state, not one of the original thirteen, was the first to be admitted to the United States?
3. How many republics are there in the U.S.S.R.?
4. Is provision for an attorney general in the Cabinet to be found in the Constitution or the Judiciary Act of 1789?
5. The symbol of a bundle of sticks tied around an axe gave its Latin name, *fasces*, to the political system of Fascism. Who first showed that whereas a single stick may be readily broken, this is not so when several are bound together in a bundle, and thus taught the lesson that "Union gives strength"?
6. As applied to legislative bodies, what is meant by cloture?
7. Can you define pornocracy?
8. What do the initials S.P.Q.R. signify?
9. Was England or the United States the first to adopt women's suffrage at the national level?
10. What has the term "Salic law" come to mean?

GOVERNMENT

1. The Bill of Rights.
2. Vermont, in 1791.
3. Fifteen.
4. In neither. The Constitution made no provision for the Cabinet, nor did the Judiciary Act. It was one of a number of precedents established by George Washington, based on the British system of government.
5. Aesop.
6. It is a parliamentary procedure for ending debate after which the matter under discussion is voted on immediately.
7. Prevalent in the Papal Court in the tenth century, pornocracy (from the Greek *porno,* prostitute, and *Krates,* strength or power) means the influence of courtesans on the government.
8. *Senatus Populusque Romanus*—"the Senate and the People of Rome."
9. England, in 1918. The United States followed in 1920.
10. A law believed to derive from the code of laws of the ancient Salic Franks, excluding females from succession to the throne. It was later used to bar women from the thrones of France and Spain.

GREAT BRITAIN

1. Identify Ben Lomond.
2. What was the name of the first Duke of Marlborough?
3. How did Rotten Row, which is now a bridle path in London's Hyde Park, get its name?
4. How are the following place names pronounced in Great Britain?

   a) Fowey
   b) Mousehole
   c) Belvoir
   d) Lympne
   e) Leominster

   f) Uttoxeter
   g) Balquhidder
   h) Ulgham
   i) Kircudbright
   j) Zwill

5. Which American institution was founded with funds provided by an Englishman who had never visited the United States?
6. Give the more common name for the Yeoman of the Guard and the Yeoman Warders at the Tower of London who wear colorful uniforms modeled after those of the Tudor period?
7. Where is London's geographical center, from which all distances to and from the capital are measured?
8. Upon what object were the sovereigns of Scotland, and now the sovereigns of Great Britain, crowned?
9. Give the American equivalents of the following British expressions:

   a) boffin
   b) winkle-pickers
   c) plonk
   d) brothel-creepers
   e) fascia

   f) bumf
   g) refer to drawer
   h) bomb (in show business)
   i) Bath Oliver
   j) Wellingtons

10. Which landowner owns the most property in Great Britain?

GREAT BRITAIN

1. Ben Lomond is a mountain which overlooks the famed Loch Lomond of song, the largest lake in Scotland.

2. John Churchill. As Duke of Marlborough, he won his greatest victory at Blenheim, in Bavaria, in 1704, putting the French under Louis XIV on the defensive. For this Queen Anne and a grateful nation built Blenheim Palace for him, one of the greatest houses and the only nonroyal palace in Great Britain.

3. It is the anglicized version of the French *Route du Roi*, "the King's Road."

4. The correct pronunciations are: a) fey b) moo-zel c) beever d) lim e) lem-ster f) uck-ster g) bal-widder h) uff-am i) ker-koo-bri j) yool

5. The Smithsonian, in Washington, which was started with funds provided by James Smithson for the establishment of an institution for the "increase and diffusion of knowledge among men." Smithson, a distinguished scientist, was the illegitimate son of the first Duke of Northumberland.

6. Beefeaters, who originally were the soldier-servants who served the king and his guests during meals. The name may derive from *buffetier du roi*, or buffeteers of the King.

7. A point just behind the statue of Charles I at Charing Cross, on the south side of Trafalgar Square.

8. The Stone of Scone, also called the Coronation Stone, underneath the seat of the throne which is only used for coronations. The throne is on display at Westminster Abbey.

9. a) research engineer or scientist b) pointed shoes c) cheap white wine (corruption of *blanc*) d) crepe-soiled suede shoes e) dashboard (of a car) f) paperwork or toilet paper g) insufficient funds h) smash hit i) a brand of dry cracker j) originally, short leather boots; now, generally rubber boots

10. The Forestry Commission.

GROVES OF ACADEME

1. Who advised us to "seek for truth in the groves of Academe"?
2. The term "little red schoolhouse" became to the early Americans a symbol of popular education. Why was it painted red?
3. What founder of a college was a brewer?
4. Who educated whom at the "College of One"?
5. Alexander the Great was fortunate in having whom as a tutor?
6. Can you name the colleges from which Presidents Kennedy, Johnson, Nixon, Ford, and Carter were graduated?
7. Which is the oldest university in the New World?
8. The "School of the Ten Bells" specializes in which delicate craft?
9. Which leading university was named after an Englishman who had amassed a fortune with the East India Company?
10. What remarkably inept student wrote the following in later years? "By being so long in the lowest form I gained an immense advantage over the cleverer boys. . . . I got into my bones the essential structure of the ordinary British sentence—which is a noble thing. Naturally I am biased in favor of boys learning English; and then I would let the clever ones learn Latin as an honor, and Greek as a treat. But the only thing I would whip them for would be for not knowing English. I would whip them hard for that."

GROVES OF ACADEME

1. Horace in Book II of his Epistles.
2. Because it was the cheapest color available. Most wooden schoolhouses are now painted white.
3. Matthew Vassar.
4. F. Scott Fitzgerald instructed Sheilah Graham, who described the experience in her book *Beloved Infidel*.
5. Aristotle.
6. Harvard, Southwest Texas State Teachers, Whittier, Michigan, and the U.S. Naval Academy, respectively.
7. Universidad de San Marcos, in Lima, Peru, founded in 1551.
8. It is a school for pickpockets. Its curriculum involves a mannequin with ten pockets in its clothing, on each of which a bell has been sewn. To graduate, the student must pick every pocket without ringing a bell.
9. Yale University, formerly the Collegiate School, changed its name in 1718 in honor of Elihu Yale, who had donated a gift of goods and books to the school. When sold, these brought £562—the largest gift to the college before 1837. Elihu Yale is buried in Wrexham, Wales.
10. Winston Churchill, *My Early Life*.

HORSES

1. What are quarter horses?
2. Can you locate a horse's fetlock? His withers?
3. What is the name of the famous winged steed in Greek mythology?
4. Who rode these horses in films: Tony, Champion, and Scout?
5. Define the terms "maiden" and "yearling" as used in horse racing.
6. What is the present location of the four bronze horses which came originally from Constantinople and were taken by Napoleon?
7. What horse won the largest amount in his racing career?
8. Winning which three races constitutes the Triple Crown? Name the first horse to win it.
9. Where would you find the line, "A horse! a horse! my kingdom for a horse!"?
10. Can you name the steeds of Alexander the Great, Don Quixote, and General Robert E. Lee?

HORSES

1. They are a breed of strong saddle horses developed in the western United States and trained for races up to a quarter of a mile. The All-American Futurity, a series of elimination races for a purse exceeding one million dollars, the richest in the world, is held for quarter horses over 440 yards at Ruidosa Downs, New Mexico.
2. The fetlock is on the back side of the leg, above the hoof. The withers are the highest part of the back, located at the base of the neck and between the shoulder blades.
3. Pegasus.
4. Tom Mix, Gene Autry, and Tonto.
5. A maiden is a racehorse that has never won a race. A yearling is a thoroughbred racehorse that is one year old or has not completed its second year.
6. On top of St. Mark's Cathedral in Venice.
7. Kelso won $1,977,896 between 1959 and his retirement in 1966.
8. The Kentucky Derby, the Preakness, and the Belmont Stakes. Sic Barton in 1919.
9. Shakespeare's *Richard III*, Act V, Scene 4.
10. Bucephalus, Rosinante, and Traveller.

HOUSE AND HOME

1. Who was the author of *A House Is Not a Home*?
2. What are lares and penates?
3. Where would an épergne be placed?
4. How did the popular Parsons table get its name?
5. Give the name of the fine glazed pottery made especially in France but originating in Italy.
6. For what is Grinling Gibbons famous?
7. Describe an oriel.
8. An ormolu object or ornamentation would have which color?
9. Do you know the original function of the drawing room?
10. Can you define the following antique terms?

   a) Chinoiserie
   b) Bisque
   c) Grandmother
   d) Coquillage
   e) Niddy noddy

   f) Cachepot
   g) Bombé
   h) Farthingale
   i) Récamier
   j) Cabriole

HOUSE AND HOME

1. Polly Adler, a notorious New York madam, who in her book "could boast a clientele culled not only from *Who's Who* and the *Social Register*, but from Burke's *Peerage* and the *Almanach de Gotha*."

2. Esteemed household possessions, from the names of the Roman household gods.

3. At the center of a table. It is a large silver or glass centerpiece.

4. Not from a clergyman, but from the Parsons School of Design, in New York, where it was developed in the 1930s.

5. Faience. The name derives from the French, short for (*vaisselle de*) *Faience*, (vessel of) Faenza.

6. Fine woodcarving. He was a master woodcarver to the crown from the reign of Charles II to that of George I, and he was often employed by Sir Christopher Wren for architectural decoration.

7. It is a projecting bay window.

8. Golden. Ormolu is imitation gold and derives from the French *or moulu*, "ground gold."

9. Originally it was the withdrawing room to which the ladies withdrew after dinner.

10. a) Imitating the Chinese.
    b) Unglazed ceramic ware.
    c) Small long-case clock.
    d) Shell-like ornamentation.
    e) Reel for winding yarn.
    f) Ornamental container for a flowerpot.
    g) Furniture with bulging front or sides.
    h) Chair with a wide seat and no arms.
    i) Couch or bed with head and feet scrolled outward.
    j) A curved leg ending in an ornamental foot.

HUMOR

Can you identify the authors of the following?

1. "Call me Ishmael. Feel absolutely free to."
2. " 'Shut up!' he explained."
3. "What's on your mind—if you'll forgive the overstatement?"
4. "Never play poker with a man named Doc and never eat at a place called Mom's.
5. "He flung himself from the room, flung himself upon his horse and rode madly off in all directions."
6. "If all the girls at the Yale Prom were laid end to end, I wouldn't be at all surprised."
7. "I was gratified to be able to answer him promptly, and I did. I said I didn't know."
8. "Yesterday morning I awoke from a deep dream of peace, compounded of equal parts of allonal and Vat 69, to find that autumn was indeed here."
9. "I believe a little incompatibility is the spice of life, particularly if he has income and she is pattable."
10. "A woman drove me to drink, and I never even had the courtesy to thank her."

HUMOR

1. Peter de Vries
2. Ring Lardner
3. Fred Allen
4. Nelson Algren
5. Stephen Leacock
6. Dorothy Parker
7. Mark Twain
8. S.J. Perelman
9. Ogden Nash
10. W.C. Fields

HUNTING AND FISHING

1. Name a great-grandson of Noah who was a mighty hunter.
2. Which sporting classic was written by Izaak Walton in the seventeenth century?
3. Doing a "Macnab" is a difficult day's work. What does it involve?
4. For what is the Restigouche noted?
5. Describe a capercaille or capercalizie.
6. How did Francis Macomber die in Hemingway's story *The Short, Happy Life of Francis Macomber*?
7. What is an arctic char?
8. Can you name the most popular gamebird in Spain?
9. For which sports in Scotland would you employ the services of a gillie?
10. Which famous book was reviewed in the following terms?

> "This fictional account of the day-by-day life of an English gamekeeper is still of considerable interest to outdoor-minded readers, as it contains many passages on pheasant raising, the apprehending of poachers, ways to control vermin, and other chores and duties of the professional gamekeeper. Unfortunately one is obliged to wade through many pages of extraneous material in order to discover and savor these sidelights on the management of a Midlands shooting estate, and in this reviewer's opinion this book cannot take the place of J.R. Miller's *Practical Gamekeeping*."

HUNTING AND FISHING

1. Nimrod (Genesis 19:8-10).
2. *The Compleat Angler or the Contemplative Man's Recreation*. Besides describing the art of angling, Walton draws a picture of peace and meditation which is in sharp contrast to the civil war raging at the time.
3. Killing a salmon, shooting a grouse, and stalking and killing a stag within twenty-four hours, having forewarned the owners that their lands would be poached. The term came from a feat described in the novel *John Macnab* by John Buchan.
4. It is a river in the province of New Brunswick, Canada, famous for its salmon fishing.
5. It is a large grouse. Its name derives from a Scottish-Gaelic word meaning "horse of the woods."
6. He was shot by his wife after showing cowardice on safari by running away from a wounded lion.
7. It is a type of trout.
8. The *perdiz*, or red-legged partridge.
9. Fishing and deer-stalking.
10. *Lady Chatterley's Lover* by D. H. Lawrence. This tongue-in-cheek review by Ed Zern appeared in the magazine *Field and Stream*.

INDIANS

1. How did the American Indians come into the Western hemisphere?
2. What celebrated error in history led to the name "Indian"?
3. Who did the Aztecs and their leader, whom we call Montezuma, believe Cortes and the Spaniards to be when they entered Mexico in 1519?
4. Whom did the Spaniards call Atahualpa?
5. What was the name of the Indian chief who was invited to dine with the Pilgrims on their first Thanksgiving in 1621 and who signed a treaty with them which he faithfully observed until his death?
6. Describe wampum and tell its uses.
7. Were the Plains Indians always nomadic?
8. Can you identify Nokomis, Daughter of the Moon?
9. At the Battle of the Little Bighorn in 1876, who wiped out Custer and his men after they rashly attacked the largest Indian encampment in the Northwest?
10. Which are the three most populous Indian tribes in the United States?

117

INDIANS

1. It is generally believed that they came from Asia via the Bering Strait in a series of migrations. From Alaska they spread east and south.

2. Columbus, like other early explorers, thought he had circumnavigated the globe and reached the Indies of Asia. He therefore named the islands he visited the West Indies, and their inhabitants Indians.

3. The descendants of their great god Quetzalcoatl.

4. He was the Inca of Peru and ruler of the Incan Empire when Pizarro and the Spaniards entered Peru in 1532. Atahualpa was executed, although he offered two rooms of gold and silver as ransom, which the Spanish accepted.

5. Massasoit, chief of the Wampanoag Indians.

6. Wampum, small cylindrical beads made from polished shells, was used both as currency and jewelry.

7. No, not until the sixteenth century, when the Spanish brought horses to North America. Prior to that, since they lacked transportation, they generally stayed close by stream beds and lakes where game was plentiful.

8. Nokomis was Hiawatha's grandmother, in Longfellow's "The Song of Hiawatha."

9. Sioux and Cheyenne warriors, headed by the Sioux Chiefs Sitting Bull and Crazy Horse. Chief Crazy Horse actually led the attack on Custer and his men.

10. In descending order, they are Navaho, Cherokee, and Sioux.

INSULTS

1. Beau Brummell, encountering the Prince Regent and a companion out for a stroll in London, made what scathing inquiry of the companion?

2. Who described Algernon Charles Swinburne as "sitting in a sewer and adding to it"?

3. What did Samuel Johnson have to say about the letters of Lord Chesterfield?

4. "The same old sausage, fizzing and sputtering in his own grease" was whose opinion of Thomas Carlyle?

5. Walking down Piccadilly one day, the Duke of Wellington was addressed by a stranger who said, "Mr. Brown, I believe?" What was the Iron Duke's reply?

6. How did Winston Churchill handle Lady Astor when she said, "If you were my husband, I'd poison your coffee."?

7. George Bernard Shaw received this invitation from a celebrity huntress: "Lady X will be at home Thursday between four and six." He returned the card, having written what on it?

8. When they were leaving by the same door, Clare Boothe waved Dorothy Parker ahead, saying, "Age before beauty." Miss Parker swept through with what apt rejoinder?

9. Who is reputed to have said, "I never forget a face, but in your case I'll make an exception."?

10. In which fashion is Churchill supposed to have knifed Clement Attlee when someone observed that he was a very modest man?

INSULTS

1. "Who's your fat friend?"
2. Thomas Carlyle.
3. The famous letters, Johnson found, teach "the morals of a whore and the manners of a dancing master."
4. Henry James.
5. "Sir, if you believe that, you'll believe anything."
6. "And if I were your husband, I should drink it."
7. "Mr. Bernard Shaw likewise."
8. "Pearls before swine."
9. Groucho Marx.
10. Churchill is said to have agreed, adding, "He has a great deal to be modest about."

ISLANDS

1. Which Mediterranean island was the seat of a high civilization in pre-Hellenic times?
2. How did the Virgin Islands get their name?
3. What is the largest noncontinental island mass in the world?
4. On which rainy island did the fanatical missionary Mr. Davidson "fall from grace" with the prostitute Sadie Thompson and as a consequence slit his throat?
5. Why are the Pacific islands of Juan Fernández remembered?
6. Byron in *Don Juan* wrote that "burning Sappho loved and sung." With which island is she associated?
7. Name the four principal Channel Islands.
8. Can you locate the islands of Langerhans?
9. Islands seem to have played an important part in Napoleon's life. Name four with which he was intimately associated.
10. What is the most remote inhabited island in the world?

ISLANDS

1. Crete.
2. When Columbus discovered the Virgin Islands, he found them so numerous that he was reminded of the legend of St. Ursula, the Virgin Martyr of Cologne, who, with her 11,000 virgin handmaidens, was murdered by Huns in the fourth century.
3. Greenland. (Australia is generally regarded as a continental land mass.)
4. Tutuila, one of the American Samoan islands, the principal town of which, Pago Pago, was the locale of W. Somerset Maugham's short story "Miss Thompson." This story was later made into a play and a film, entitled *Rain*.
5. After a quarrel with his captain in 1704, Alexander Selkirk, a Scottish sailor, asked to be put ashore here. He was picked up four years later, and his adventures suggested to Daniel Defoe the story of *Robinson Crusoe*, which appeared in 1719.
6. The Greek island of Lesbos, from which the word "lesbian" comes.
7. Jersey, Guernsey, Alderney, and Sark.
8. They are insulin-producing cells in the pancreas, the malfunction of which causes diabetes.
9. Corsica, where he was born; the Île de la Cité in Paris, where he became Emperor; Elba, to which he was exiled; and St. Helena, where he died.
10. Tristan da Cunha, in the South Atlantic. The nearest land is St. Helena, some 1,300 miles to the northeast.

JAZZ

1. Where was Storyville, and what part did it play in the early history of jazz?
2. Explain the term "tailgate trombone."
3. Who was the "Empress of the Blues"?
4. Which prolific jazz musician held sacred music concerts in Grace Cathedral, San Francisco, and in the Cathedral of St. John the Divine in New York?
5. Who has been called the "King of Ragtime"?
6. Who was the first jazz man to recruit band members purely on the basis of musical ability, without regard for race?
7. Which famous jazz club was named after the father of modern jazz? Who was he?
8. What was unusual about the guitarist Django Reinhardt?
9. A new market for jazz as a concert form was exploited by which group? Who played alto saxophone?
10. Which singer has performed with virtually every major jazz musician?

123

JAZZ

1. It was the legendary red-light district of New Orleans, consisting of a 38-block area, where many of the early jazz bandleaders appeared in the sporting houses. Its closing by the Navy in 1917 had the effect of dispersing jazz musicians and their talents throughout the country.
2. This was the style of playing trombone in New Orleans and takes its name from the location of the trombonist on a horse-drawn parade cart, where he would have ample room to operate the trombone slide.
3. Bessie Smith.
4. Duke Ellington.
5. Scott Joplin.
6. Benny Goodman.
7. Birdland. Charlie ''Yardbird'' Parker.
8. He had only three fingers on his left hand and was a gypsy.
9. The Dave Brubeck Quartet. Paul Desmond.
10. Ella Fitzgerald.

KITH AND KIN

1. Whose grandmother was eaten by a beast?
2. Who lived with Uncle Henry and Aunt Em?
3. Which president was the grandfather of another president?
4. George McManus originated which famous comic strip featuring a successful Irish immigrant and his parvenu wife?
5. Who wished his wife "to be not so much as suspected"?
6. Can you name the March sisters of literature?
7. Who was the original Uncle Sam whose name became the national symbol of the United States, and what was his business?
8. Who stood on his head, somersaulted, devoured an entire goose, and balanced an eel on the end of his nose?
9. Which two ladies served poisoned elderberry wine to elderly gentlemen?
10. What do Ann Landers and Abigail Van Buren have in common?

KITH AND KIN

1. Little Red Riding Hood, in the well-known tale translated from the French of Perrault.
2. Dorothy, in L. Frank Baum's *The Wonderful Wizard of Oz*.
3. William Henry Harrison was the grandfather of Benjamin Harrison.
4. "Bringing up Father", with Jiggs and Maggie.
5. Julius Caesar, according to Plutarch's *Lives*. This is the origin of the traditional saying that Caesar's wife must be above suspicion.
6. Jo, Meg, Beth, and Amy, in *Little Women*, by Louisa May Alcott.
7. Samuel Wilson, a meat-packer from Troy, New York, who was called "Uncle Sam" by his employees. During the War of 1812, the initials "U.S." stamped on food containers for the armed forces were jokingly said to stand for "Uncle Sam".
8. Father William, from the verse in Lewis Carroll's *Alice's Adventures in Wonderland*.
9. The Brewster sisters, Aunt Abby and Aunt Martha, in the play *Arsenic and Old Lace*, by Joseph Kesselring.
10. They are twin sisters who write popular "advice" columns.

LAST WORDS

Can you identify the people who uttered these dying words?

1. Calling for champagne, he said, "I am dying, as I have lived, beyond my means."
2. "The executioner is, I believe, very expert, and my neck is very slender."
3. As he considered himself a burden to his companions, he walked out of the tent in a blizzard, saying, "I am just going outside and may be some time." He never returned.
4. "Well, what *is* the answer?" A long pause. Then: "But what, then is the question?"
5. To his First Captain: "Kiss me, Hardy. Thank God I have done my duty." It has been conjectured that he might have said, "Kismet, Hardy."
6. "Turn up the lights. I don't want to go home in the dark."
7. In reply to a suggestion that Queen Victoria come to his death-bed: "Why should I see her? She will only want to give a message to Albert."
8. "Only one man ever understood me." Then, after a pause: "And he didn't understand me."
9. To his doctor who suggested that the salt air at the seaside town of Bognor Regis might be beneficial: "Bugger Bognor!"
10. "It has all been very interesting."

LAST WORDS

1. Oscar Wilde, 1854-1900, the Irish poet, wit, and dramatist.
2. Anne Boleyn, 1507-1536, second wife of Henry VIII.
3. Lawrence E.G. Oates, 1880-1912, a member of the Scott expedition to the South Pole. On the return journey, they all perished.
4. Gertrude Stein, 1874-1946, American author and patron of the arts.
5. Horatio, Viscount Nelson, 1758-1805, English admiral and hero of the Battle of Trafalgar.
6. William Sidney Porter ("O. Henry"), 1862-1910, American short-story writer.
7. Benjamin Disraeli, first Earl of Beaconsfield, 1804-1881, British statesman and author.
8. Georg Wilhelm Friedrich Hegel, 1770-1831, German philosopher.
9. Attributed to King George V of England, 1865-1936.
10. Lady Mary Wortley Montagu, 1689-1762, English author noted for her highly descriptive letters.

LAW

1. What is the difference between libel and slander in common law?
2. Explain the Marvin Doctrine. For whom was it named?
3. What is *habeas corpus*?
4. Who proclaimed that "the law is a ass, a idiot"?
5. Which principle was upheld in the trial of John Peter Zenger?
6. Can you state the substance of Parkinson's Law?
7. Who is the chief justice of the Supreme Court?
8. Explain the difference between robbery and larceny.
9. In law, what is meant by double jeopardy?
10. Murphy's Laws are justifiably famous. Can you give two out of three?

LAW

1. Libel is written, printed, or mechanically broadcast, while slander is only spoken.
2. According to the California courts, a discarded mistress (in this case movie actor Lee Marvin's) has virtually the same rights as a wife.
3. The writ issued to bring a person before a court or judge to determine that there has been no unlawful restraint.
4. Mr. Bumble, in Charles Dickens' *Oliver Twist*.
5. The publisher's acquittal helped to establish the principle of freedom of the press in the thirteen colonies.
6. Parkinson's Law states: "Work expands to fill the time available for its completion." This law was enunciated by Professor C. Northcote Parkinson in an article published in *The Economist* of London in 1955 after investigating the British Admiralty and the Colonial Office.
7. There is no longer such a title. There is, however, a chief justice of the United States, who is one of the nine members of the Supreme Court.
8. Robbery is theft in which force or fear is used; larceny is theft in which neither is used.
9. Being put on trial twice for the same offense. Double jeopardy is outlawed by the Bill of Rights.
10. Murphy's Laws have been codified as follows:

    a) Nothing is as easy as it looks.
    b) Everything will take longer than you think it will.
    c) If anything can go wrong, it will.

THE LONG AND THE SHORT OF IT

1. How long is an eon?
2. Where did short-horn cattle originate?
3. Who wrote *Tales of a Wayside Inn*?
4. Just how short is a short wave?
5. Name the pirate leader in Stevenson's *Treasure Island*.
6. Which seventeenth-century English philosopher described the life of man as "solitary, poor, nasty, brutish and short"?
7. Whose autobiographical masterpiece was *Long Day's Journey into Night*?
8. Who was of the opinion that "Short words are best and the old words when short are best of all."?
9. What is the longest word in the unabridged *Oxford English Dictionary*?
10. Can you name seven short men who were engaged in the mining business?

THE LONG AND THE SHORT OF IT

1. An eternity.
2. In northern England, where they are also called Durham cattle.
3. Henry Wadsworth Longfellow.
4. It is an electromagnetic wave with a wavelength of 80 meters or less.
5. Long John Silver.
6. Thomas Hobbes, in *Leviathan*.
7. The American playwright Eugene O'Neill.
8. It was a saying of Winston Churchill's.
9. Floccinaucininihilipilification, which is the action or habit of estimating as useless.
10. Doc, Happy, Grumpy, Dopey, Sleepy, Sneezy, and Bashful, in Walt Disney's classic *Snow White and the Seven Dwarfs*.

McMACS

1. As used in surnames, what do "Mc" and "Mac" indicate?
2. The abbreviation "M.C." might represent what five descriptive terms?
3. The resistance to the British bombardment of what fort inspired Francis Scott Key to do what?
4. Name an important body of water closest to the Ross Ice Shelf in Antarctica.
5. To which two men do we owe the names for a type of surfaced road and of a raincoat?
6. Why is Ray A. Kroc one of the richest men in the United States?
7. In Japan a shogun was a military leader who exercised absolute rule. Who has been nicknamed the last shogun?
8. Who said, "Lay on, Macduff, / And damn'd be him that first cries, 'Hold, enough!' "?
9. Which English historian and statesman was one of two powerful forces in shaping the distinctive prose style of Winston Churchill?
10. To Alfred Hitchcock, what is the McGuffin?

McMACS

1. Son of.

2. Marine Corps, Medical Corps, Member of Congress, Military Cross, or Master of Ceremonies.

3. The successful defense of Fort McHenry in Baltimore against the British naval assault in 1814 inspired Key to write what is now our national anthem, *The Star-Spangled Banner*, on the morning following the bombardment.

4. McMurdo Sound.

5. John McAdam, a Scottish engineer, for the macadam road, which consisted of layers of compacted small stones, now usually bound with tar or asphalt; and Charles Macintosh, a Scottish chemist, who developed a raincoat of patented rubberized cloth.

6. He is the founder and Senior Chairman of the Board of the McDonald's hamburger chain.

7. General Douglas MacArthur, who from 1945 to 1951 was commander of the occupying forces of the Allied Powers in Japan and directed the occupation of the country.

8. Macbeth.

9. Thomas Babington Macaulay. The other strong influence on Churchill's style was Edward Gibbon, who wrote *The History of the Decline and Fall of the Roman Empire*.

10. The motive force in his films; or the "secret" everyone is intent on keeping or revealing.

MAGIC AND THE OCCULT

1. Can you explain the connection between the wise men from the East of the Nativity story and magicians?
2. How many cards are there in the tarot deck used in fortunetelling?
3. What is a familiar? Can you give the name of the familiar that appeared in John van Druten's play *Bell, Book and Candle*?
4. Name the prophetess in Greek legend whose predictions, though true, were never believed.
5. What are jumbies?
6. Do you know the legend of the witch who was nicknamed "Cutty Sark"?
7. In what poem would you find these lines?

    It was down by the dark tarn of Auber,
    In the ghoul-haunted woodland of Weir.

8. Who was Erich Weiss, and what was his contribution to magic?
9. Of what are the leprechauns of Ireland inordinately fond?
10. Complete the Scottish prayer which begins "From ghoulies and ghosties."

MAGIC AND THE OCCULT

1. The wise men were also called the Magi. This is the plural of the Persian word *magus*, or sorcerer, from which the word magician is derived.
2. Seventy-eight cards, 56 of which are called the *Minor Arcana* and the remaining 22 the *Major Arcana*.
3. An attendant spirit which often takes animal form. A Siamese cat called Pyewacket.
4. Cassandra, a daughter of Priam, King of Troy.
5. To the natives of the West Indies, they are zombies, or the living dead.
6. In his poem "Tam o'Shanter" Robert Burns tells of a country boy fleeing a pursuing witch who was clad only in a *cutty sark* (a mini-skirt in Scots dialect). Knowing that witches cannot follow over water, he rode his mare over a bridge. Nevertheless, "Cutty Sark" did succeed in snatching the mare's tail. The figurehead of Britain's famed tea clipper Cutty Sark, now preserved at Greenwich on the Thames, is a bare-breasted young woman in a cutty sark, with a mare's tail in her outstretched hand. A well-known brand of Scotch whiskey takes its name from the clipper ship.
7. "Ulalume," by Edgar Allan Poe.
8. Weiss was the real name of Harry Houdini, who took his stage name after the noted French magician Houdin. Houdini was a master in the art of escape and also exposed fake mediums.
9. Whiskey and tobacco.
10. "And long-leggety beasties and things that go bump in the night, Good Lord, deliver us!"

MANNERS AND MORES

1. Who wrote a book, subtitled *The Blue Book of Social Usage*, which featured such personages as the Mmes. Kindhart, Toplofty, Wellborn, and Cravin Praise; the Oldnames, the Upstarts, the Highbrows, and the Onceweres; "Bobo" Gilding, and Constance Style; Mr. Stocksan Bonds, Jim Smartlington, the genial Clubwin Doe, and that archbounder Richan Vulgar?

2. What are the magic expressions of etiquette?

3. At a church wedding, why is it customary for the bride to take the right arm of her father?

4. In setting the table for a formal dinner, should one place the napkin to the left or right of the place setting?

5. Should you be presented to the Queen of England, what is the correct form to be observed?

6. After the ladies have withdrawn from the dinner table, to which direction should the gentlemen pass the port?

7. When a man is walking with a lady in the city, why is it considered polite for him to take the curb side of the pavement?

8. In which countries is it correct to belch following a meal?

9. With which hand do the Arabian desert nomads eat?

10. Speech may, or may not, be a "mirror of the soul," in the words of Publilius, yet it is by one's speech that one is most readily known. The words and phrases that follow are generally considered to be in bad taste, pretentious, or, in the memorable usage popularized by Nancy Mitford, "Non-U" ("U" standing for upper-class speech). Give the correct form for the following:

   a) Pleased to meet you   g) Wealthy
   b) Pardon me   h) Formals
   c) Elegant home   i) Drapes
   d) Lovely food   j) Serviette
   e) Boy (when over 21)   k) Corsage
   f) I desire to purchase   l) Passed away

MANNERS AND MORES

1. Emily Post, the author of *Etiquette*.
2. "Please" and "Thank you."
3. Because this enables the father to reach the front pew on the left (the bride's side) without crossing the bride's train.
4. Neither. The napkin should be folded flat and laid on each "place" plate.
5. You should never initiate conversation. When replying, however, you should use in the first instance the title "Your Majesty," and subsequently "Ma'am."
6. To the left.
7. The custom dates from the Middle Ages, when slops were emptied from the windows of the houses onto the street below. The person walking farthest from the street had less chance of being hit.
8. In China and Japan and many of the Pacific nations, where it is a sign of appreciation for the food.
9. Only the right, the left being considered unsanitary because of its associations with eliminative functions. (It will be apparent, in this context, why having one's hand cut off is one of the ultimate degradations in the Arab world.)
10. The following terms are considered "U" as opposed to "Non-U":

    a) How do you do! Or, I am very glad to meet you.
    b) I beg your pardon. Or: Excuse me! Or: Sorry!
    c) Beautiful house, or place
    d) Good food
    e) Man
    f) I should like to buy
    g) Rich
    h) Dinner jacket or black tie
    i) Curtains or, possibly, draperies
    j) Dinner napkin
    k) Flowers to wear
    l) Died

MEDICINE

1. What is rhinoplasty?
2. When should the Heimlich maneuver be used on a person?
3. When would a doctor use a trepan?
4. In what campaign did Dr. Paul Ehrlich's "magic bullet" play an important part?
5. What is a placebo, and what does it literally mean?
6. What is the best cures for circadian disrythmia?
7. What is the "king's evil"?
8. Who was Dr. Philip Syng Physick?
9. What kind of doctor was Frankenstein?
10. Do you know the origin of the phrase "Caesarean section," for the delivery of a baby by abdominal incision?

MEDICINE

1. Plastic surgery of the nose.

2. When the person is choking on food. To dislodge the food, you stand behind the victim, then make a fist with one hand and place the fist at the top of the victim's abdomen, just under the rib cage. Grasp your fist with the other hand and give a quick upward thrust. Slapping someone on the back should be avoided, as it only aggravates the choking problem.

3. In brain surgery. A trepan is a crown, or cylindrical, saw for perforating the skull.

4. The war against syphilis. Dr. Ehrlich discovered salvarsan, which proved effective in the treatment of the disease.

5. A substance with no medication, given simply to humor a patient. In Latin *placebo* means "I shall please."

6. Rest probably. The term circadian disrythmia (Latin *circa,* about, and *dies,* day) means jet lag, or the disruption of bodily rhythms by rapidly changing time zones.

7. Scrofula, a skin disease which the touch of a reigning monarch is supposed to cure.

8. A pioneer American surgeon who studied in Edinburgh and was the first professor of surgery at the University of Pennsylvania.

9. He was not a doctor, nor even a medical student. His fields of study were natural science and mathematics.

10. It is certainly not derived from Julius Caesar, who had a normal birth. The phrase probably had its origin in the Latin *a caeso matris utere*, "from the incised womb of his mother," from *caesus*, past participle of *caedere*, "to cut."

140

MEETINGS

1. Who had a historic meeting at Ujiji?
2. Which representatives of the "Big Three" (Great Britain, Russia, and the United States) met at the Potsdam Conference in the summer of 1945, following Germany's defeat in World War II?
3. Where do the Society of Friends regularly get together?
4. These lines open which well-known play?
   When shall we three meet again?
   In thunder, lightning, or in rain?
5. Sherlock Holmes was destined to have his last meeting with his archenemy Professor James Moriarty at what spot on the Continent?
6. Who wrote, "Oh, East is East, and West is West, and never the twain shall meet."?
7. What German phrase means "Till we meet again"?
8. Where does the Blue Nile meet the White Nile?
9. Who was the author of the touching play *Still Life*, later made into a film titled *Brief Encounter*?
10. Where do "I have a rendezvous with Death," according to Alan Seeger, a poet who achieved fame in World War I?

MEETINGS

1. It was here on the shores of Lake Tanganyika in 1871 that Henry Morton Stanley uttered the memorable words "Dr. Livingstone, I presume," on encountering the famous Scottish missionary and explorer for whom he had been searching.
2. Prime Ministers Attlee and Churchill, Marshal Stalin, and President Truman. (Attlee replaced Churchill as Prime Minister midway through the conference.)
3. At Meeting. The name "Quaker" is probably derived from the admonition of George Fox, founder of the Society, to "tremble at the word of the Lord."
4. Shakespeare's *Macbeth*.
5. According to Dr. Watson in "The Final Problem," they last met on a precipice over the Reichenbach Falls, near Meiringen, Switzerland, where in the course of a struggle they both appeared to have fallen into the "dreadful cauldron of swirling water," presumably to their deaths. Holmes, however, miraculously reappeared to continue his adventures.
6. Rudyard Kipling, in "The Ballad of East and West."
7. *Auf Wiedersehen*.
8. The two great rivers have their confluence at Khartoum, the capital of the Republic of Sudan.
9. Noël Coward.
10. "At some disputed barricade."

MENU NOTES

1. As a first course hors d'oeuvres are always appropriate. What does the term literally mean?

2. How did the term "Newburg" for a type of seafood dish, such as Lobster Newburg, come into being?

3. On a Scottish menu you might find Cock-a-Leekie, Arbroath Smokies, and Atholl Brose. What are these dishes?

4. Whose chef first served Chicken Marengo?

5. Can you translate *Hasenpfeffer mit Kartoffelpuffer*, which might appear on the menu of a Munich restaurant?

6. The famous chef Escoffier while working at the *Hôtel de Paris* in Monaco, created a special dessert for a noted Australian soprano. What was it, and who was she?

7. Why might *Omelette Norvégienne* be a nice touch to conclude a dinner at Lasserre in Paris?

8. Or perhaps you would prefer the multilayered pastry called a napoleon. How did its name arise?

9. To go with any or all of the above, you could do worse than to order two bottles of "The Widow" '69, which the *sommelier* would interpret as what?

10. On supper menus as a savory the familiar melted cheese on toast dish appears variously as "Welsh Rarebit" and "Welsh Rabbit." Which is the correct spelling?

MENU NOTES

1. "Outside the works"—that is, before the main course.

2. This dish was originally called Seafood Wenberg after Ben Wenberg, a New York shipping merchant who invented it and supplied the cayenne, a vital ingredient. It first appeared at the renowned Delmonico's in New York. After an argument with Wenberg, Delmonico renamed the dish "Newberg" by transposing the first three letters of Wenberg. The word now is generally spelled "Newburg."

3. Chicken and leek soup, smoked haddock, and a cream and whisky-flavored pudding.

4. Napoleon's chef, from the ingredients at hand following the Battle of Marengo in northwestern Italy in 1800, when Napoleon defeated the Austrians.

5. It is a rich hare stew with potato pancakes.

6. Peach Melba, after Dame Nellie Melba. (Melba Toast was also named in her honor.)

7. It is Baked Alaska (ice cream covered with meringue and browned in the oven).

8. The pastry is of Italian origin and is a corruption of *napolitain*. It has nothing whatsoever to do with the emperor.

9. Veuve Clicquot—a fine dry champagne of the 1969 vintage. (*Veuve* means "widow" in French.)

10. Welsh Rabbit. It is a humorous phrase, playing on the poverty of the Welsh. Through failure to understand the joke, writers of cookbooks generally called the dish "Welsh Rarebit." Contrary to the general view, Welsh Rabbit is not a corruption of Rarebit, but rather the reverse is true. As Fowler says in *Modern English Usage*: "Welsh Rabbit is amusing and right, and Welsh Rarebit is stupid and wrong."

MIND OVER MATTER

1. Who was Psyche?
2. Of a psychiatrist, a psychologist, and a psychoanalyst, who needs to be a licensed physician?
3. Who is regarded as the father of psychoanalysis?
4. What phenomenon has been explored scientifically on a large scale by J.B. Rhine, of Duke University?
5. From which organ of the body is the word "hysterical" derived?
6. Name the psychological test which uses the subject's interpretation of a series of abstract designs to analyze personality traits.
7. Can you differentiate between the ego and the id?
8. For which type of psychology is Carl Gustav Jung noted?
9. Will Schutz is a behavioral psychologist whose first book, *Joy*, introduced which contemporary idea?
10. How many of the following fancies and fears can you identify?

    a) Acrophobia   f) Dromomania
    b) Ailuromania   g) Stygiophobia
    c) Ergophobia   h) Eleutheromania
    d) Agoraphobia   i) Gynephobia
    e) Monophobia   j) Pantophobia

MIND OVER MATTER

1. In classical mythology, she was the maiden who was loved by Eros. The name personified the soul. In medical terminology, the prefix "psych-" means the mind.
2. A psychiatrist.
3. Sigmund Freud.
4. Parapsychology, which includes the study of such psychic phenomena as clairvoyance, telepathy, psychokinesis and extrasensory perception.
5. The uterus, from the Greek word *hystera*. Since women were considered more unstable than men, it was believed that hysteria must be caused by some purely female organ.
6. The Rorschach test.
7. According to Freud, the ego is the conscious mind, which rules one's behavior, while the id is the unknown and unconscious mind.
8. Analytical psychology, emphasizing the importance of racial and cultural inheritance to a person's development.
9. The encounter group, to develop awareness and encourage nonverbal communication.
10. a) Fear of heights
    b) Love of cats
    c) Morbid fear of working
    d) Fear of open spaces
    e) Fear of being alone
    f) Compulsive traveling
    g) Fear of Hell
    h) Mad zeal for freedom
    i) Abnormal fear of women
    j) Fear of everything

MISTRESSES

1. Whose mistress was originally a peasant girl and later an empress?
2. What did Evelyn Nesbit cause?
3. Why is the name Mayerling remembered?
4. Which British Prime Minister started his letters to his mistress, and later wife, Frances Stevenson, with "My Darling Pussy"?
5. Who became Napoleon's mistress in an attempt to save Poland?
6. The actress Marion Davies was the mistress of which famous newspaper publisher?
7. What was the occupation of Nell Gwynn, the paramour of Charles II?
8. Which wonderfully descriptive term has been applied to Emilienne E'Alçenon, Liane de Pougy, La Belle Otèro, and other *grandes cocottes* of *La Belle Époque*, as the decade of the 1890s in Paris was known?
9. According to Robert Service's poem, who worked at the Malamute saloon and was the light-o'-love of Dangerous Dan McGrew?
10. George Romney became famous for his portraits of the beautiful mistress of which celebrated naval commander?

MISTRESSES

1. Peter the Great, who married Catherine I of Russia.
2. The murder of her lover, the famed architect Stanford White by her husband, the playboy Harry K. Thaw.
3. It was at a hunting lodge (now a convent) at Mayerling that Archduke Rudolf, heir to the Austro-Hungarian throne, and his mistress, Maria Vetsera, met their mysterious deaths in 1889.
4. Lloyd George.
5. Countess Maria Walewska.
6. William Randolph Hearst.
7. Once an orange-seller at the Theatre Royal, she became an actress.
8. "Grand Horizontals," whose affairs were described by Cornelia Otis Skinner in her book *Elegant Wits and Grand Horizontals*.
9. "The lady that's known as Lou."
10. Horatio, Viscount Nelson. Romney painted Emma, Lady Hamilton.

MONEY

1. According to the Bible, what is "the root of all evil"?
2. Why are the edges of gold and silver coins milled?
3. From what is our word "dollar " derived?
4. Whose picture appeared on the face of the highest denomination of U.S. paper currency to be circulated publicly, and what denomination was this?
5. What was called "Seward's Folly" and how much did it cost the United States?
6. The term "Dixie," for the South, had what monetary origin?
7. With which countries are the following currencies associated: schilling, sol, won, quetzal, dirham, and baht?
8. Who observed that no one ever went broke by underestimating the taste of the American public?
9. Can you distinguish between the two terms used for the basic money supply of the United States—M1 and M2?
10. What was the observation of the fabulously rich Nubar Gulbenkian, an Englishman of Armenian extraction, on his custom-built London taxicab, which was tall enough for him to sit in without removing his top hat?

MONEY

1. Not money, but "the love of money." (I Timothy 6:10)
2. So that it will be apparent if any metal has been filed or cut away.
3. It comes from the German *thaler*, which is short for *Joachim-staler*, an early Germanic coin, minted from silver mined in St. Joachim's Valley.
4. Salmon P. Chase, former Secretary of the Treasury and Chief Justice, appeared on the $10,000 bill. (All bills higher than $100 are now being withdrawn from circulation.)
5. William Seward was the Secretary of State who negotiated the purchase of Alaska from the Russians in 1867 for $7.2 million. It was also called "Seward's Icebox" and "Seward's Polar Bear Garden."
6. When Louisiana became a state, bilingual ten-dollar bills were printed with *dix* ("ten" in French) on one side. These bills were called dixies, and the term originally applied to New Orleans. The popularity of the song "Dixie" expanded the term to include all of the South.
7. Austria, Peru, South Korea, Guatemala, Morocco and United Arab Emirates, and Thailand, respectively.
8. P. T. Barnum, American showman.
9. M1 consists of cash in public hands and checking accounts. M2 includes M1 plus all private deposits except those large ones represented by certificates. These measures are considered important economic determinants.
10. "They tell me it turns on a sixpence, whatever that is."

MONTHS OF THE YEAR

1. Which month is literally two-faced?
2. An epithet for Juno, the Roman goddess of marriage and fertility, gives us the name of which month?
3. How did the expression "mad as a March hare" originate?
4. Why is April a perfect time for love?
5. The prologue of which famous work begins with these lines?

   When that Aprill with his shoures soote
   The droghte of March hath perced to the roote . . .

6. According to Sir Thomas Malory in *Morte d'Arthur*, which is the "lusty month"?
7. In whose honor are June and July named?
8. Give the title of the best-selling book about World War I by Barbara W. Tuchman.
9. Walter Huston sang "September Song" in which Broadway show, by whom?
10. September, October, November, and December are literally the seventh, eighth, ninth, and tenth months respectively. How did this arise?

MONTHS OF THE YEAR

1. January, which comes from Janus, the Roman god for gates and doors, who was always represented on Roman coins as facing in two directions at once. This enabled him to gaze on both the past and the future at the same time.

2. February, from *Februaria*. At this time of year the Romans engaged in a curious celebration, which involved running around and striking women with sacred thongs so that they would not be barren. The name for these thongs was *februa*, or "instruments of purification."

3. Because March is supposedly the mating season of hares, although some observers have noted that hares know no season. March is named for Mars, the Roman god of war, since the month was ideal for warfare.

4. Its name came into Latin from the Greek *Aphro*, a shortened form of Aphrodite, the goddess of love.

5. *The Canterbury Tales* by Geoffrey Chaucer. It is written in what is known as Middle English.

6. May: "For it giveth unto all lovers courage, that lusty month of May." Or, in the words of Willard R. Espy ("Mr. Anonymous"):

   "Hooray! Hooray! The first of May!
   Outdoor fucking starts today!"

   The name is believed to derive from Maia, a goddess of spring.

7. June, the traditional month for marriage, is consecrated to Juno, while July is dedicated to Julius Caesar. The name was suggested by Mark Antony as it was Caesar's birthday month, and it came into use in the same year that Caesar was assassinated.

8. *The Guns of August* (World War I became general in August, 1914). The name of the month came from Augustus Caesar, otherwise known as Octavian, the first Roman emperor, and the adopted son and heir of Julius Caesar.

9. *Knickerbocker Holiday*, by Maxwell Anderson and Kurt Weill.

10. Because the Roman New Year began with the month of March.

152

MOVIES

1. What was the first all-talking feature picture, and in what year did it appear?
2. Who said, "Beulah, peel me a grape," and in what film?
3. Who spoke the last words in *Gone With The Wind*, and what were they?
4. What did the films *Edward, My Son, Rebecca,* and *The Great Man* have in common?
5. Who played the part of the bank inspector J. Pinkerton Snoopington in the W.C. Fields movie *The Bank Dick*?
6. Which actress was the top box office draw during World War II?
7. Can you complete the line "Play _____, Sam" from *Casablanca* and tell who said it? What was the title of the song referred to, and who played it?
8. One of the trademarks in films directed by Alfred Hitchcock is the walk-on nonspeaking appearance of Hitchcock himself. How did he accomplish this in *Lifeboat*, when the setting was a lifeboat holding the few survivors of a torpedoed ship?
9. Who is the only movie star to appear on a postage stamp?
10. A star's name is often made, not born. Do you know the screen names of the following?

   a) William Beedle
   b) James Stewart
   c) Norma Jean Mortensen
   d) Reginald Truscott-Jones
   e) Issur D. Demsky
   f) Frances Gumm
   g) Marion M. Morrison
   h) Anna Maria Italiano
   i) Frederick Austerlitz
   j) Allen Stewart Konigsberg

MOVIES

1. *Lights of New York*, in 1928.
2. Mae West, in *She Done Him Wrong*.
3. Vivien Leigh, as Scarlett O'Hara, closed the film, saying, "After all, tomorrow is another day."
4. The title characters never appeared on the screen.
5. Franklin Pangborn.
6. Betty Grable.
7. "Play it, Sam." (Not "Play it again, Sam.") The words were spoken by Ingrid Bergman, not Humphrey Bogart. "As Time Goes By" was played and sung by Dooley Wilson.
8. His picture was shown in a before-and-after reducing advertisement in a newspaper held by one of the survivors.
9. Grace Kelly, on the stamps of Monaco commemorating her marriage to Prince Rainier IV in 1956.
10. a) William Holden
    b) Stewart Granger
    c) Marilyn Monroe
    d) Ray Milland
    e) Kirk Douglas
    f) Judy Garland
    g) John Wayne
    h) Anne Bancroft
    i) Fred Astaire
    j) Woody Allen

MUSIC

1. A sackbut was the early name for which musical instrument?
2. What are the four movements of a symphony, which Haydn developed into the classical standard?
3. The words of Yale's "Whiffenpoof Song" were adapted from which poem by a famous English author?
4. Which musician surrendered his wife to his best friend, who was a famous composer?
5. How many keys are there on a standard piano?
6. Who was the composer of the hymn "Onward, Christian Soldiers"?
7. What is an *eisteddfod*, and where does it occur?
8. Who has been called history's most justifiably neglected composer, who had enough daring and ignorance to write for both the double reed slide music stand and the left-handed sewer flute simultaneously, using their incompatibility as a structural element in the composition?
9. To the tune of what song was "The Battle Hymn of the Republic" set?
10. Can you fill in the following blanks? As an example, the answer to "Vincent Lopez _____" is "Vincent Lopez and His Casa Lopez Orchestra."

    a) Les Brown

    b) Al Horlick

    c) Shep Fields

    d) Fred Waring

    e) Kay Kyser

    f) Glen Gray

    g) Bob Crosby

    h) Guy Lombardo

    i) Horace Heidt

    j) Phil Spitalny

MUSIC

1. The trombone.
2. *Allegro, andante, scherzo, finale.*
3. "Gentleman Rankers," from Rudyard Kipling's *Barrack Room Ballads.*
4. Hans von Bülow, to Richard Wagner, who fathered two children by Cosima von Bülow.
5. Eighty-eight—52 white, 36 black.
6. Sir Arthur Sullivan, of Gilbert and Sullivan fame.
7. An *eisteddfod* is a Welsh competitive festival in which contests with special emphasis on music and poetry are held.
8. P. D. Q. Bach, the last and unquestionably the least of the great Johann Sebastian Bach's many children, whose definitive biography has been written by Prof. Schickele. Among his many works deserving of obscurity is Pervertimento in C major for strings, bagpipes, bicycles, and balloons.
9. That of "John Brown's Body."
10. a) and His Band of Renown
    b) and His A & P Gypsies
    c) and His Rippling Rhythm
    d) and his Pennsylvanians
    e) and His College of Musical Knowledge
    f) and his Casa Loma Orchestra
    g) and The Bobcats
    h) and His Royal Canadians
    i) and His Musical Knights
    j) and His All Girl Orchestra, featuring Evelyn and Her Magic Violin

MYTHOLOGY

1. In the Trojan War, what ruse did the Greeks employ to enter the city of Troy?
2. What are the great texts of Icelandic mythology called?
3. What are talaria, and who wore them?
4. Who was Europa?
5. A certain sea god, who had the power to change shapes, gives us what adjective which applies to anyone who changes his mind or opinions easily, to suit the circumstances?
6. Who was the nymph whose unrequited love for Narcissus caused her to pine away until nothing but her voice remained?
7. Can you describe the particular piece of equipment that Procrustes used on his victims to make them measure up?
8. Which god is usually depicted playing a syrinx, or shepherd's pipe?
9. Who were the Aesir?
10. Can you name five of the nine Muses and the art or science over which each presided?

MYTHOLOGY

1. They built a large hollow wooden horse in which a small group of warriors was concealed. At night, after the Trojans had taken the horse within the city walls, the warriors crept out of the horse, opened the city gates for the Greek army, and Troy was sacked.
2. Eddas.
3. Winged sandals such as those worn by Hermes and Iris, as represented in Greco-Roman painting and sculpture.
4. A Phoenician princess abducted to Crete by Zeus in the guise of a white bull.
5. Protean, from Proteus.
6. Echo.
7. A bed, on which he put all those who fell into his hands. If they were too tall to fit it exactly, he cut them down to size; if they were too short, he stretched them to fit.
8. Pan, the Greek god of woods, fields, and flocks, who has a human torso with goat's horns, ears, and legs. The word "panic" derives from Pan, who could arouse terror in lonely places.
9. The gods of Norse mythology, from the Old Norse, plural of $\overline{ass}$, meaning god.
10. Calliope, epic poetry; Clio, history; Erato, love poetry; Euterpe, music; Melpomene, tragedy; Polyhymnia, sacred poetry; Terpsichore, dance; Thalia, comedy; Urania, astronomy.

NAMES ON THE MAP

1. After whom is the Caribbean Sea named?
2. What prompted the Italian explorer Amerigo Vespucci, when sailing along the northern coast of South America in 1499, to give it the name Venezuela?
3. Apart from both being in Africa, what do the Sahara Desert and Lake Nyasa have in common?
4. Can you name Tamerlane's capital?
5. In 1513 Ponce de Leon named a group of islands after the Spanish for "shallow water." What do we know them as today?
6. The names of many cities in the United States—Annapolis, Indianapolis, Minneapolis—contain the suffix *polis*, which means what in Greek?
7. The former French territory of Afars and Issas is now which independent state on the Horn of Africa?
8. The Netherlands means literally what?
9. In 982 Eric the Red sailed west from Iceland and reached the shores of an island further north. Why did he name it Greenland when it was far colder and less hospitable than the island he had left?
10. What European city is famous for a cathedral containing the shrine of the Magi and for a scent it produces?

NAMES ON THE MAP

1. After the fierce Carib Indians, who inhabited the islands of the area.

2. When he encountered native villages built on wooden piles in the shallow water, he was reminded of Venice, and so he named this area "little Venice," or Venezuela.

3. Since Sahara is from the Arabic word *Sahra*, meaning desert, and since Nyasa is a corruption of the Bantu word *nyanza*, meaning lake, the Sahara Desert and Lake Nyasa are Desert Desert and Lake Lake, respectively.

   (Lake Nyasa has been known as Lake Malawi since 1965.)

4. Samarkand.

5. The Bahamas, from the Spanish *baja mar*.

6. City.

7. Djibouti.

8. Lowlying lands.

9. By giving it a lush-sounding name, he hoped to attract settlers.

10. Cologne, Germany.

NAVAL AND NAUTICAL LORE

1. Do you know the Latin origin for the word "captain"?
2. Who had "the face that launched a thousand ships, and burnt the topless towers of Ilium," in the words of Marlowe?
3. Why were black neckerchiefs adopted by British sailors?
4. In honor of whom did John Paul Jones name his ship *Bonhomme Richard*?
5. A watch at sea is normally for a four-hour period, with the half-hour periods being noted by the ship's bell ringing from one to eight. How did this practice come about?
6. Which is the oldest commissioned ship in the U.S. Navy?
7. What was the port side of a ship originally called, and why was the name changed?
8. During the Civil War the first battle in history between two iron-clad vessels took place. What were their names?
9. What is a scuttlebutt, and why does the word mean rumor or gossip?
10. Between the Allied landings in North Africa in November 1942 and the invasion of Sicily in July 1943, which was the only U.S. naval unit in offensive action in the Mediterranean?

NAVAL AND NAUTICAL LORE

1. The Latin word *caput*, meaning "head."

2. According to Greek mythology, it was Helen, wife of King Menelaus of Sparta. Her abduction by Paris brought on the Trojan War.

3. To keep the tarred pigtails of the sailors from soiling their uniform collars.

4. Benjamin Franklin. The "Richard" is taken from Franklin's popular publication *Poor Richard's Almanack*.

5. Because the passage of time was originally noted by a half-hour glass.

6. The U.S.S. *Constitution*. Commissioned and put to sea in 1798, she is now maintained in Boston.

7. Larboard. It was changed because of its similarity in sound to starboard. (The "star" in starboard derives from the Anglo-Saxon *steor*, meaning rudder.)

8. Not the *Monitor* and the *Merrimack*, but the *Monitor* (North) and the *Virginia* (South). The latter was originally called the *Merrimack* when it was abandoned by the North, but was renamed when taken by the South and rebuilt. The battle between the two ships ended in a draw. Their ironclad design, however, was to revolutionize naval warfare.

9. A cask with a bunghole cut in it, kept on deck to hold water for drinking. It was here that sailors would gather to exchange the latest rumor.

10. Eighteen PT Boats of Motor Torpedo Boat Squadron Fifteen.

OPENERS

Listed below are the opening lines from a number of famous English and American literary works. How many authors and titles can you identify?

1. "Call me Ishmael."
2. "Much have I travell'd in the realms of gold."
3. "Come live with me and be my love."
4. "He was born with the gift of laughter and a sense that the world was mad."
5. "Go and catch a falling star, / Get with child a mandrake root."
6. "In the year 1878 I took my degree of Doctor of Medicine of the University of London."
7. "One thing was certain, that the *white* kitten had had nothing to do with it—it was the black kitten's fault entirely."
8. "He did not wear his scarlet coat / For blood and wine are red."
9. "Virginia, your little friends are wrong."
10. "It is a truth universally acknowledged that a single man in possession of a good fortune must be in want of a wife."

OPENERS

1. Herman Melville, *Moby-Dick*.
2. John Keats, "On First Looking into Chapman's Homer."
3. Christopher Marlowe, "The Passionate Shepherd to His Love."
4. Rafael Sabatini, *Scaramouche*.
5. John Donne, "Song."
6. Arthur Conan Doyle, *A Study in Scarlet*.
7. Lewis Carroll, *Through the Looking-Glass*.
8. Oscar Wilde, *"The Ballad of Reading Gaol"*.
9. Francis Pharcellus Church, Editorial: "Is There a Santa Claus?", first published in the *New York Sun*, September 21, 1897, in reply to an inquiry from Virginia O'Hanlon.
10. Jane Austen, *Pride and Prejudice*.

OPERA

1. Can you give the derivation of the word *opera*?
2. What operas are comprised in the "Nibelungen Ring Cycle" of Wagner?
3. Why is the term "Savoyards" given to the performers in the Gilbert and Sullivan operettas?
4. What kind of factory did Carmen work in?
5. Who observed that "Of all the noises known to man, opera is the most expensive"?
6. In what opera does the aria "La Donna è Mobile" occur? How would you translate it?
7. Who composed *Die Fledermaus*? *The Merry Widow*?
8. In which opera is there a famous "Mad Scene"?
9. Name the operas in which these well-known choruses are sung: Anvil, Pilgrims', Soldiers'.
10. In which of Gilbert and Sullivan's works would you hear the following sung?

    And everyone will say,
    As you walk your mystic way,
    If this young man expresses himself
    In terms too deep for *me*,
    What a very singularly deep young man
    This deep young man must be!

OPERA

1. *Opera* derives from the Latin *opus*, meaning "work"; *opera*, or "works," is the plural. It is a shortened form of the Italian phrase for a musical drama, *opera in musica*.
2. *Das Rheingold, Die Walkure, Siegfried, Die Götterdämmerung*.
3. Because these operettas were originally performed by the D'Oyly Carte Company at the Savoy Theatre in London.
4. A cigarette factory.
5. Molière, the French playwright and actor.
6. *Rigoletto*, by Giuseppe Verdi. "The lady is fickle."
7. Johann Strauss, the younger. Franz Lehar.
8. *Lucia di Lammermoor*, by Gaetano Donizetti.
9. *Il Trovatore* by Verdi. *Tannhäuser* by Wagner. *Faust* by Gounod.
10. *Patience*, an operetta ridiculing the aesthetic movement.

OSCARS

The Academy of Motion Picture Arts and Sciences, which was founded in 1927 with Douglas Fairbanks as its first president, began the distribution of their coveted Academy Awards in 1929. These golden statuettes have been called "Oscars" since 1931.

1. The first Academy Award for Best Picture went to which film?
2. Who won more Oscars than any other person?
3. The only Academy Award made of wood was given to whom?
4. Only one actor has won Oscars for Best Actor and Best Supporting Actor. Can you name him and the pictures involved?
5. Who is the only performer to be nominated 11 times for an Academy Award and to win three Oscars for starring roles?
6. What do the following have in common: Walter Huston, Kirk Douglas, Judy Garland, Ryan O'Neal, and Henry Fonda?
7. Who has refused to accept an Oscar?
8. Which performer managed to win Academy Awards for playing three parts in two films?
9. Is it possible for an X-rated film to win an award for Best Picture?
10. Name the two actors who have received the most nominations as best actor.

OSCARS

1. *Wings*, a film about the early days of aviation, featured Richard Arlen, Clara Bow, Charles "Buddy" Rogers, and Gary Cooper.
2. Walt Disney, with a total of 31 Oscars, excluding scientific or technical awards.
3. Edgar Bergen (and Charlie McCarthy).
4. Jack Lemmon, for his roles as a confused businessman in *Save the Tiger* and as an inept ensign in *Mister Roberts*.
5. Katharine Hepburn. She won Oscars for *Morning Glory, Guess Who's Coming to Dinner*, and *The Lion in Winter*.
6. They are all parents of Oscar winners: John Huston, for direction and screenplay of *The Treasure of the Sierra Madre*; Michael Douglas, as producer of *One Flew Over the Cuckoo's Nest*; and Liza Minnelli, Tatum O'Neal, and Jane Fonda as performers.
7. George C. Scott, for *Patton*, and Marlon Brando for *The Godfather*. (Sasheen Littlefeather refused it for Brando.)
8. Frederic March, for his roles in *Dr. Jekyll and Mr. Hyde* and *The Best Years of Our Lives*.
9. Yes. *Midnight Cowboy*, which won in 1969, was X-rated. (It was given an R-rating in 1971.)
10. Spencer Tracy and Laurence Olivier, who are tied at nine each.

PAINTING

1. "An Arrangement in Grey and Black" is the title of what famous painting?
2. Which leading impressionist was a close relative of the president of the Pennsylvania Railroad?
3. Describe a maulstick.
4. Whose painting of a sunrise was responsible for the term "Impressionism", which was used derisively at the time?
5. Who wrote a novel based on the life of the French painter Paul Gauguin?
6. What organ did Vincent van Gogh cut off at Christmas time and give to Rachel, a girl in a *maison de tolérance* (a licensed brothel)?
7. Do you know the more familiar names of Sanzio, Vecellio, and Buonarroti?
8. Where do Lawrence's "Pinky" and Gainsborough's "Blue Boy" face each other?
9. Which American painter became President of the Royal Academy in London?
10. Who wrote this passage?

> I must say I like bright colours. . . . I rejoice with the brilliant ones, and am genuinely sorry for the poor browns. When I get to heaven I want to spend a considerable portion of my first million years in painting, and so get to the bottom of the subject. But then I shall require a still gayer palette than I get here below. I expect orange and vermilion will be the darkest, dullest colours upon it, and beyond them there will be a whole range of wonderful new colours which will delight the celestial eye."

PAINTING

1. Whistler's portrait of his mother.
2. Mary Cassatt, the sister of Alexander J. Cassatt.
3. It is a long wooden stick used by painters to support the hand that holds the brush.
4. Claude Monet whose painting was titled "Impression, Sunrise")
5. W. Somerset Maugham, *The Moon and Sixpence*.
6. His right ear.
7. Raphael, Titian, and Michelangelo, respectively.
8. At the Huntington Library and Art Gallery in San Marino, California.
9. Benjamin West.
10. Winston S. Churchill in *Painting as a Pastime*.

PAIRS

1. Which famous pair of lovers were brought together by a lascivious intermediary named Pandarus, from whom the word "pander" is derived?
2. According to legend, who were suckled by a she-wolf and later founded what great city?
3. What would you need to visit the Biblical ruins of Sodom and Gomorrah?
4. What is the legend of Pygmalion and Galatea, and what famous musical was based on it?
5. Who were Chang and Eng?
6. Who strolled along the beach and later dined famously on bread and oysters, with pepper and vinegar?
7. Can you name the title characters from *The Two Gentlemen of Verona* in Shakespeare's play?
8. Why is it terrible to be caught between Scylla and Charybdis?
9. What did the intensively-studied families of the Jukes and the Kallikaks have in common?
10. For what profession did Burke and Hare provide a particular service?

PAIRS

1. Troilus and Cressida, whose romance has been told by Boccaccio, Chaucer, and Shakespeare.
2. The twins, Romulus and Remus. Rome.
3. Diving equipment, since if they exist, they lie buried under lava and the Dead Sea.
4. Pygmalion, a king of Cyprus, hated women but sculpted a statue of such beauty that he fell in love with it. Aphrodite brought the statue to life as Galatea. *My Fair Lady*, by Lerner and Loewe, from the play *Pygmalion* by George Bernard Shaw.
5. The most famous of conjoined twins, they were born in Siam of Chinese parents in 1811 and were known as the Siamese Twins when they were exhibited in P.T. Barnum's circus. Later they married and fathered 22 children.
6. The Walrus and the Carpenter, from *Through the Looking-Glass*, by Lewis Carroll.
7. Valentine and Proteus.
8. Because by avoiding one, you invite destruction by the other. In Greek mythology they were personified as female monsters who were often a peril to mariners. In reality Scylla is a huge rock off the toe of Italy, and across the Strait of Messina is Charybdis, a whirlpool off the Sicilian coast.
9. Feeble-mindedness, with a high incidence of crime and disease. The names were pseudonyms for two U.S. families which were studied to determine the influence of heredity.
10. The medical profession. They were celebrated grave robbers who provided the medical schools of Edinburgh with fresh cadavers for anatomical study. They not only robbed graves but also smothered living victims to ensure fresh delivery

PEACE

1. What are the origins of the dove and olive branch as peace symbols?
2. Who used a calumet?
3. Describe the Peacemaker.
4. The phrase "ignoble peace" was coined by whom?
5. Which war was terminated by the peace treaty signed in 1905 at Portsmouth, New Hampshire?
6. What was Henry Ford's contribution to peace during World War I?
7. Many peace treaties were signed in Paris. Those signed there in 1763, 1783, 1856, and 1898 ended which wars?
8. What is ironic about the Nobel Peace Prize, awarded annually to further the cause of international peace?
9. Name the statesman whose confident line "Peace for our time," after he signed the Munich Pact with Hitler in 1938, came to haunt the advocates of appeasement.
10. Which two armistices were signed in a railroad car in the forest of Compiègne, in France?

PEACE

1. They come from the Book of Genesis in the Bible. There it is said that Noah sent forth a dove from the ark to see if the waters had abated, and the dove returned with an olive leaf in its mouth, indicating that the flood was over and thus that the anger of God was appeased.

2. The North American Indians. It is a long-stemmed, ornamental pipe used for ceremonial purposes and was also known as a "peace pipe."

3. The 1873 Colt single-action pistol, which was a favorite of the Western gunfighters.

4. Theodore Roosevelt, in *The Strenuous Life*.

5. The Russo-Japanese War.

6. In 1915 he headed a peace expedition to Europe, which proved to be a dismal failure.

7. The Seven Years War, the War of American Independence, the Crimean War, and the Spanish-American War, respectively.

8. Alfred Nobel, a Swedish chemist and manufacturer invented dynamite, although he later had strong misgivings about the potential use of his invention in warfare.

9. The British Prime Minister Neville Chamberlain.

10. Hitler forced the French to sign the armistice of June 1940, in the same car where the armistice ending World War I in 1918 was signed.

PHILOSOPHY

1. Its Greek roots give what meaning to the word "philosophy"?
2. Which famous Greek philosopher always wrote in the form of a dialogue, and who was his teacher?
3. What was the "Philosopher's Stone"?
4. Which philosopher and mathematician coined the phrase, *"Cagito ergo sum"* (I think, therefore I am)?
5. Name the authors of *System of Logic* and *Critique of Pure Reason*.
6. The words "epicure" and "epicurean" have a connotation of "eat, drink, and be merry". Is this in keeping with the teaching of the Greek philosopher, Epicurus, from whom the words are derived?
7. Which doctrine maintains that the value of any external fact or possession or experience depends on the way in which we take it?
8. Give the name of Sir Thomas More's most famous work, one which contributed a new word to the English language.
9. What was the philosophic and literary movement that flourished in New England in the nineteenth century and led its thinkers to the mystical belief in individualism and the harmony of all things in nature?
10. Which French writer is a leading exponent of twentieth-century existentialism, whereby man is free and totally responsible for what he makes of himself?

PHILOSOPHY

1. The love of wisdom, from *philos*, love, and *sophia*, wisdom.
2. Plato. Socrates.
3. A mineral sought by alchemists, that would transmute base metals into gold.
4. René Descartes in *Le Discours de la Méthode*
5. John Locke and Immanuel Kant, respectively.
6. No. Although Epicurus defined philosophy as the art of making life happy, with pleasure as the highest and only good, he did not consider pleasure as heedless indulgence but the opposite, with serenity manifesting itself in the avoidance of pain. As a man, Epicurus was extremely frugal and was ordinarily satisfied with bread and water.
7. Stoic self-control by law.
8. *Utopia*, from the Greek for "nowhere." More envisaged a land of perfection in social, moral, and political life.
9. Transcendentalism.
10. Jean-Paul Sartre.

PHRASE ORIGINS

Can you give the probable source of the following phrases or expressions?

1. To peter out
2. Fit to a T
3. Scarce as hens' teeth
4. To read the riot act
5. Straight from the horse's mouth
6. Not a Chinaman's chance
7. Flaming youth
8. To pull strings
9. Stark-naked
10. Holy Toledo!

PHRASE ORIGINS

1. This phrase, meaning to diminish gradually or to become exhausted, is probably an allusion to Peter's action after Jesus was seized in the Garden of Gethsemane. Before dawn Peter thrice denied that he ever knew Jesus.

2. This expression comes from the T-square used by draughtsmen for establishing and drawing parallel lines.

3. Pretty scarce, since hens have no teeth.

4. In England there actually was a Riot Act, signed by George I in 1716, which was directed against unlawful assembly of twelve or more persons. The penalties were severe, ranging upward to life imprisonment.

5. Receiving information in this manner is getting it on the highest authority, in the same way that the only sure way of telling a horse's age is by examining its teeth.

6. This refers to the slim chance for survival the Chinese laborers had in the early days of the California gold rush, when they were ignorant of American ways and unable to speak the language.

7. Not Scott Fitzgerald, but William Shakespeare, when he says in *Hamlet*: "To flaming youth let virtue be as wax, / And melt in her own fire."

8. This phrase for using influence to gain an advantage comes directly from the marionette show, where the person behind the curtain pulls strings or wire to control the movement of the puppets.

9. In this phrase "stark" is a corruption of the Anglo-Saxon *steort*, meaning "rump" or "tail." So to be stark-naked is to be literally bare-assed.

10. This expression refers to Toledo, Spain which became a great Christian center after the expulsion of the Moors.

PICK A NUMBER

1. How many wives did Henry VIII have? Can you name them?
2. What is a baker's dozen, and how did the phrase come about?
3. John Buchan wrote a thrilling spy novel, later made into a movie, which had what numerical title?
4. Can you give within 104 miles the circumference of the earth at the equator?
5. Which world-famous restaurant is known by its numerical address?
6. In A.E. Housman's famous poem, how old was the Shropshire lad who heard a wise man say the following?

   "Give crowns and pounds and guineas
   But not your heart away . . ."

7. How many years elapsed between the Declaration of Independence and Lincoln's Gettysburg Address?
8. What is the Pentateuch?
9. Within two hours, how long was Lindbergh's flight to Paris on March 21, 1927?
10. How many birds were received in the song "The Twelve Days of Christmas"?

PICK A NUMBER

1. Six. Katharine of Aragón, Anne Boleyn, Jane Seymour, Anne of Cleves, Catherine Howard, and Catherine Parr.
2. Thirteen. In England during the Middles Ages it became customary, to avoid the harsh penalties for short-weighing bread, to give the customer thirteen loaves for every dozen ordered.
3. *The 39 Steps*.
4. 24,896 miles.
5. The "21" Club, at 21 West Fifty-second Street in New York City, originally started as a speakeasy in 1922 by Jack Kriendler and Charlie Burns, it was known for years as "Jack and Charlie's.
6. "When I was one-and-twenty". The poem ends:

   And I am two-and-twenty
   And ah, 'tis true, 'tis true.
7. 87 years ("Four score and seven years ago . . .").
8. The first five books of the Old Testament.
9. 33 hours, 29 minutes.
10. Twenty-three: 1 partridge, 2 turtledoves, 3 French hens, 4 calling birds, 6 geese, and 7 swans. (Also received were 5 gold rings, 8 maids a-milking, 9 ladies dancing, 10 lords a-leaping, 11 pipers piping, and 12 drummers drumming.)

PLANTS AND TREES

1. What is the oldest living thing on earth? The largest?
2. Who was known as the "Plant Wizard"?
3. Which plant is supposed to shriek when it is torn from the earth?
4. The dried bark of a South American evergreen tree provides which drug used in the cure and prevention of malaria?
5. From which country does an ornamental tree called the ginkgo come?
6. Can you give the end products of photosynthesis?
7. How did Socrates meet his end?
8. Which plant, greatly prized by the Chinese for a variety of medicinal purposes, has branched roots resembling the human form?
9. Under which parasitic shrub is kissing encouraged?
10. Which World War I poet concluded his most famous work as follows?

    Poems are made by fools like me,
    But only God can make a tree.

PLANTS AND TREES

1. A bristlecone pine named "Methuselah," in California, with a confirmed age of 4,600 years. A sequoia called "General Sherman," in California's Sequoia National Park. It stands 270 feet high.
2. Luther Burbank, the American horticulturist.
3. The mandrake.
4. Quinine.
5. China.
6. Carbohydrates and oxygen.
7. Charged with corrupting the youth of Athens, he was forced to drink a poison prepared from the European water hemlock.
8. Ginseng.
9. Mistletoe.
10. Joyce Kilmer, "Trees."

POLITICAL LEADERS

1. Who was first called "The Father of His Country"?
2. Who is the leader of the party advocating secession of Quebec from Canada?
3. Can you identify Don José Hidalgo?
4. What concert pianist became premier of his country?
5. What British Prime Minister's efforts to redeem fallen women were the despair of his family and friends?
6. Who is called "the Liberator" in South America?
7. What is the more familiar name of Lord Beaconsfield?
8. To whom did Napoleon refer as "shit *(merde)* in a silk stocking"?
9. Who was Dzhugashvili?
10. Who characteristically wrote in the preface to his book: "Every great movement on this globe owes its rise to the great speakers and not to the great writers."?

POLITICAL LEADERS

1. Cicero.
2. René Lévesque, head of the *Parti Québécois*.
3. He was a humble parish priest who is regarded as the father of Mexican independence.
4. Ignace Paderewski, one of the greatest concert pianists of all time, was premier of Poland in 1919 and 1940-41 (the latter period in exile).
5. William Gladstone.
6. Simón Bolívar.
7. Disraeli.
8. Talleyrand.
9. Stalin.
10. Adolf Hitler, in *Mein Kampf*.

THE PRINTED WORD

1. Who was the first person to print in English?
2. What is the motto of the *New York Times* and who coined it?
3. What was Winston Churchill's assignment in the Boer War?
4. Can you name the largest building in the world devoted entirely to rare books and manuscripts?
5. Who said, "No man but a blockhead ever wrote except for money."
6. Who wrote the play (later a movie) *The Front Page*?
7. Which weekly magazine has the largest circulation in the world? Which monthly magazine?
8. In which American cities are the following newspapers located? the *Blade*, the *Plain Dealer*, the *Post-Intelligencer*, and the *Times-Picayune*?
9. Name the famous flier who worked for *The Daily Planet*.
10. In which city is the oldest Russian newspaper in the world published?

THE PRINTED WORD

1. William Caxton in the 15th century. His translation from the French in 1475, *The Recuyell of the Historyes of Troye*, was the first book printed in English.
2. "All the News That's Fit to Print," coined by Adolph S. Ochs who was publisher of the paper from 1896 to 1935.
3. He was sent to cover it in 1899 as a correspondent for a London newspaper, the *Morning Post*. His dispatches about his capture and imprisonment by the Boers, and subsequent escape, brought him fame at an early age.
4. The Beinecke Rare Book and Manuscript Library at Yale University.
5. Dr. Samuel Johnson in Boswell's *Life of Johnson.*
6. Ben Hecht and Charles MacArthur.
7. *TV Guide. The Reader's Digest.*
8. Toledo, Cleveland, Seattle and New Orleans.
9. Clark Kent, otherwise known as Superman.
10. *Novoye Russkoye Slovo* (New Russian Word), which was founded in 1910, is published in New York. (Papers that existed in Russia in 1917 were all shut down by the Revolution and new ones began.)

QUARTETS

1. What are the allegorical figures of the Four Horsemen of the Apocalypse in the Bible supposed to represent?
2. Of the original thirteen states, which are originally styled commonwealths?
3. How did plus fours get their name?
4. Can you explain the meaning of the four *H*'s in the 4-H clubs, which are organizations for boys and girls in rural communities?
5. Ghosts appear in which four of Shakespeare's plays?
6. Who coined the term "the four hundred" for the upper crust of fashionable society?
7. In a speech to Congress in 1941 proposing lend-lease legislation, President Roosevelt enunciated the principle of the Four Freedoms, which was later incorporated in the Atlantic Charter. What are the Four Freedoms?
8. Can you give the derivation of the term "fourflusher" for a braggart or a bluffer?
9. Who was the first man to run a mile in under four minutes?
10. In the *Rubáiyát of Omar Khayyám*, what do "*Rubáiyát* and *Khayyám mean*?

QUARTETS

1. It is believed that the rider on the white horse represents Christ; the rider on the black horse is famine; on the red horse is war; and on the pale horse, death.

2. Maryland, Massachusetts, Pennsylvania, and Virginia. Each is called a commonwealth because the word was used in the original royal charter.

3. Plus fours were a style of knickerbockers which had four inches added to each leg. They were popular for golf in the twenties.

4. This is found in the club's pledge: "My Head to clearer thinking, my Heart to greater loyalty, my Hands to larger services, and my Health to better living . . ."

5. *Hamlet, Macbeth, Julius Caesar*, and *Richard III*.

6. Ward McAllister, a New York society arbiter at the end of the last century. Four hundred is believed to refer to the number that Mrs. Astor's ballroom could accommodate.

7. Freedom of speech and expression, freedom of worship, freedom from want, and freedom from fear.

8. The term arises from a poker player with a four-card flush (also called a bobtail flush), bluffing by pretending to have a full flush.

9. Roger Bannister, who in 1954 ran the mile at Oxford in 3 minutes, 59.4 seconds.

10. Quatrains and tentmaker.

RELIGION

1. What is the name of the month that Moslems fast?
2. Which is the oldest major formal religion still practiced?
3. What is the Jewish New Year called?
4. In which tongue did Jesus speak?
5. Can you describe Quetzalcoatl and state who worshipped him?
6. What and where is the Kaaba?
7. Who is eligible for election to the papacy?
8. Who was the only Englishman to become Pope?
9. Can you name the aboriginal religion of Japan which is marked by the veneration of nature spirits and of ancestors?
10. Are the letters IHS a Latin contraction of *Iesus Hominum Salvator*, "Jesus Savior of men"; *In Hoc Signo* (*Vinces*), "In this sign (thou shall conquer)"; or *In Hac Cruce Salus*, "In this (cross) is salvation."

189

RELIGION

1. Ramadan.
2. Hinduism. Its Vedic precursor was brought to India by Aryans about 1500 B.C.
3. Rosh Hashanah.
4. Aramaic.
5. A feathered serpent who was the ancient god of the Toltecs, and later the Aztecs, in Mexico.
6. It is the most sacred sanctuary, the center of the Moslem world, and the chief goal of pilgrimage. It is a small building in the court of the Great Mosque of Mecca, nearly cubic in shape, built to enclose the Black Stone which is the most venerated Moslem object, said to have been given to Abraham by the archangel Gabriel. Followers of Mohammed face toward it when praying.
7. Any baptized Roman Catholic male.
8. Nicholas Breakspear who became Pope Adrian IV in 1154. In the course of his papacy, he gave Ireland to Henry II of England.
9. Shinto, which means in Japanese "the way of the gods."
10. None of these. IHS is the symbol or monogram of Jesus, from IHSOUS, which is Jesus in Greek capitals.

REPTILES AND AMPHIBIANS

1. What is the longest and heaviest of all snakes?
2. Which are the only two poisonous lizards in the world?
3. What reptile group protects its nest, eggs, and young for up to three years?
4. Who eulogized a particular toad in a song beginning as follows?

    The world has held great Heroes,
       As history books have showed;
    But never a name to go down to fame
       Compared with that of Toad.

5. How often does a snake shed its skin?
6. Who was catapulted into fame by his story of the jumping frog "Dan'l Webster"? Dan'l is defeated when the owner of a rival frog pours quail-shot down his gullet.
7. What is the name of the third eyelid, common to reptiles and birds, which moves horizontally across the eye?
8. When a snake sticks out its tongue, what is it doing?
9. Who admired the fertile turtle in the following lines?

    The turtle lives 'twixt plated decks
    Which practically conceal its sex.
    I think it clever of the turtle
    In such a fix to be so fertile.

10. The term "crocodile tears" resulted from the belief that crocodiles weep after eating their victims, and came to mean false tears or an insincere display of grief. What is rather fishy about all this?

REPTILES AND
AMPHIBIANS

1. The anaconda, or python, of South America. One specimen shot on the upper Orinoco River measured over 37 feet.
2. The Gila monster and the Mexican beaded lizard.
3. The crocodile family.
4. The subject of the song, Mr. Toad himself, in *The Wind in the Willows*, by Kenneth Grahame.
5. Young snakes may shed as many as 14 times a year, while older ones may only shed from three to four times a year.
6. Mark Twain. The sketch was the title piece of a series of stories that formed his first book, *The Celebrated Jumping Frog of Calaveras County*.
7. The nictitating membrane.
8. Smelling.
9. Ogden Nash, in "The Turtle," from *Many Long Years Ago*.
10. Crocodiles are unable to shed tears as they have no tear glands. Secretions keep their eyes moist.

R.I.P.

1. Who lies in Grant's Tomb?
2. Whose epitaph is *"Si monumentum requiris, circumspice"* (If you seek his monument, look around), and why is it so apt?
3. In which "corner of a foreign field that is forever England" is the author of this line buried?
4. What is the significance of the carving of a lion biting the end of a sword on the tomb of King John?
5. Where does John Brown's body lie "a-mouldering in the grave"?
6. For what is King Mausolus chiefly remembered?
7. Which small island is called "the burial-place of kings" and is said to contain the remains of 48 Scottish monarchs, including Macbeth and Duncan, the king he murdered?
8. Who is the only president buried in Washington, D.C.?
9. According to Ariel in Shakespeare's *The Tempest*, where is Ferdinand's father?
10. Who lies "under bare Ben Bulben's head" with this epitaph in his own words?

> Cast a cold eye
> On life, on death.
> Horseman, pass by!

R.I.P.

1. President and Mrs. Grant.
2. Sir Christopher Wren's on his tomb in St. Paul's Cathedral, of which he was the architect.
3. Rupert Brooke died aboard ship in 1915 while serving in the Dardanelles Expedition. He is buried on the island of Skiros, one of the Sporades in the Aegean. Above his tomb is a nude male statue symbolizing youth.
4. It refers to the Magna Carta, by which the barons curbed the power of the king.
5. North Elba, N.Y. at the John Brown Farm State Historic Site, which is near Lake Placid in the Adirondack Mountains.
6. He gave his name to the mausoleum which originated with the magnificent monument erected by his wife, Queen Artemisia, in his memory. Its remains are in the British Museum.
7. Iona, one of the Inner Hebrides, off the western coast of Scotland.
8. Woodrow Wilson, in the National Cathedral. (Taft and Kennedy are buried in Arlington National Cemetery, in Virginia.)
9. "Full fathom five thy father lies."
10. William Butler Yeats. The epitaph is taken from Yeats's poem "Under Ben Bulben."

ROCK AND COUNTRY MUSIC

1. Unlike jazz, swing, and rock 'n' roll, which trace their roots back to Africa, where do the origins of country and western lie?
2. Which famous rock performer of the fifties was known as "The Hillbilly Cat," and who was the first to record him?
3. Who owns Velvet Apple Music?
4. Identify Richard Starkey and Robert Allen Zimmerman.
5. Name a famous country and western song, which became nationally popular, that was about a hobo.
6. Bill Haley and the Comets reached Number One on the charts in 1955 with a song that was introduced to many through the film *The Blackboard Jungle*. What was its title?
7. What is unusual about Ronnie Milsap and Roy Orbison?
8. Which rock festival had the largest attendance?
9. In which prisons did Johnny Cash record live albums?
10. Name the only independent R & B based firm, founded after World War II, which has survived to become a major record company.

ROCK AND COUNTRY MUSIC

1. In the British, Scottish, Welsh, and Irish folk songs.
2. Elvis Presley. Sam Phillips, founder of Sun Records, who was also the first to record Carl Perkins, Johnny Cash, Jerry Lee Lewis and Roy Orbison.
3. Dolly Parton.
4. These are the real names of Ringo Starr and Bob Dylan.
5. Roger Miller's "King of The Road."
6. "Rock Around the Clock," which was one of the first original rock 'n' roll hits by a white artist.
7. They are blind.
8. An estimated 600,000 attended "a day of music in the country" at Watkins Glen, New York in 1973. A torrential rainstorm following the concert resulted in a monumental traffic jam.
9. Folsom and San Quentin, in California.
10. Atlantic Records.

ROCKS

1. To which apostle did Jesus give the nickname of "Rock"?
2. Describe the fabulous roc.
3. What is the only rock that can be woven?
4. Name the most popular American illustrator of the twentieth century, specializing in scenes from everyday life drawn in a humorous fashion.
5. Which large American company is associated with a well-known Mediterranean landmark?
6. Give the next line after: "The breaking waves dashed high."
7. Name the battle where Stonewall Jackson was given his sobriquet.
8. A florid style of ornamentation, characterized by elaborate curved lines and popular in Europe in the eighteenth century, is called what?
9. Can you define "living stone"?
10. What is the name of the eruptive rock, also called "blue ground," from which the bulk of the world's diamonds is found?

ROCKS

1. Simon Peter (from Greek *petros*, "rock"), to whom Jesus said, "Thou art Peter, and upon this rock I will build my church."
2. It is a legendary white predatory bird of enormous size and strength which played a large part in the adventures of Sindbad the Sailor, according to Sir Richard Burton's translation of the *Arabian Nights' Entertainments*.
3. Asbestos.
4. Norman Rockwell.
5. The Prudential Insurance Company, through its advertisements showing the Rock of Gibraltar.
6. "On a stern and rock-bound coast." (From "The Landing of the Pilgrim Fathers," by Felicia Dorothea Hemans.)
7. The first battle of Bull Run (Manassas to the Confederates), where General T. Jackson and his brigade were described as standing "like a stone wall."
8. Rococo.
9. "Living stone" is stone sculpture left in its natural surroundings, as opposed to quarried stone.
10. Kimberlite, named after the city of Kimberley in South Africa.

ROMANCE AND CHIVALRY

1. What was the Holy Grail?
2. How did the Holy Grail come to Europe?
3. How did the knights of the Round Table know Galahad should seek the Grail?
4. What English courtly poet has shaped our memory of the tale of Arthur?
5. What modern poet reconstructed the tale of Arthur, and in what work?
6. What nation was ruled by Charlemagne?
7. What famous defeat of the forces of Charlemagne was immortalized in the *Chanson de Roland*? In the poem, the victors were Saraçens; in fact, they were the fiercely independent Basques.
8. What is meant by the peers of Charlemagne?
9. What forest used by the knights was later used by Shakespeare? What is its actual name?
10. Who was the knight *"sans peur et sans reproche"*?

ROMANCE AND CHIVALRY

1. The vessel from which Christ drank at the Last Supper.
2. It was brought by Joseph of Arimathea, who was said to have received it at the Last Supper.
3. Because he was able to sit in the Siege Perilous.
4. Thomas Malory.
5. Alfred, Lord Tennyson, in *Idylls of the King*.
6. The Franks.
7. Roncesvalles in the Pyrenees.
8. Twelve knights who were of equal rank and were called paladins or knights of the palace.
9. The forest of Arden. The forest of Ardennes, France.
10. The Chevalier Bayard (*c*. 1474-1524).

ROYALTY

1. Which is the oldest ruling house in the world?
2. Where did King Kamehameha rule?
3. Who was the Visigoth king who sacked Rome in 410 A.D.?
4. What relation was Louis XIV to Louis XV?
5. Of which country is King Bhumibol Adulyadej the ruler?
6. Who was Queen Geraldine?
7. Which ruler used a garden for a chessboard and dancing girls as chess pieces?
8. Who met a tragic end at Querétaro in Mexico?
9. Identify Queen Noor.
10. Can you describe the Empress of Blandings?

ROYALTY

1. That of Japan. Emperor Hirohito is the one hundred twenty-fourth in line from the first Emperor, Jimmu, who is believed to have ruled around the time of Christ.
2. He became in 1810 the first ruler over all the Hawaiian Islands, which were previously governed by warring chiefs.
3. Alaric I.
4. Great-grandfather.
5. Thailand.
6. She was the Hungarian-American countess Geraldine Apponyi, who married King Zog of Albania in 1938.
7. Akbar, Mogul emperor of India in the sixteenth century.
8. Emperor Maximilian of Mexico, who was shot there by the followers of Benito Juárez in 1867. He was the brother of Franz Josef, the Austro-Hungarian monarch.
9. She is the American, Elizabeth Halaby, who was married to King Hussein of Jordan in 1978.
10. The empress of Blandings was a prize sow belonging to the Earl of Emsworth of Blandings Castle and was described by P.G. Wodehouse in a number of stories as resembling "a captive balloon with ears and a tail".

SAINTS AND SINNERS

1. Petite Miquelon and Grande Miquelon are two of three French islands off the coast of Newfoundland. What is the third?
2. Name the seven deadly sins.
3. Which literary figure is customarily depicted in a drawing with a halo above his head?
4. Who was "more sinn'd against than sinning"?
5. What are the correct names for two Caribbean islands commonly called St. Kitts and Statia?
6. Give the author of this epigram titled *On His Books*:

   When I am dead, I hope it may be said:
   "His sins were scarlet, but his books were read."

7. What happened to St. Christopher, the patron saint of travelers, in 1969?
8. What are the four cardinal virtues?
9. Can you name the famous jazz song that became popular for funeral marches in New Orleans?
10. Where would you be likely to sin with Elinor Glyn, a writer of torrid love stories in the 1920s?

SAINTS AND SINNERS

1. St. Pierre.
2. Pride, lust, envy, anger, covetousness, gluttony, and sloth.
3. Simon Templar, in the *Saint* books, by Leslie Charteris.
4. King Lear.
5. St. Christopher (British) and Sint Eustatius (Dutch).
6. Hilaire Belloc.
7. His name was dropped from the liturgical calendar.
8. Prudence, justice, temperance, and fortitude.
9. "When the Saints Go Marching In."
10. Most probably on a skin if we can believe the following:

> "Would you like to sin
> With Elinor Glyn
> On a tiger skin?
> Or would you prefer
> To err with her
> On some other fur?"

SCIENCE

1. Who invented bifocal glasses?
2. What is the significance of the numbers 2, 10, 18, 36, 54 and 86, which identify a certain aristocratic family? The first three are loners.
3. Who was the chemist noted for his researches with wine, beer, and milk?
4. What is the most abundant metal in the earth's crust?
5. For whom is the centigrade scale named?
6. Which law of physics states that for every action there is an equal and opposite reaction?
7. Which metal is named after a goblin?
8. Can you state in words one of Einstein's basic equations, $E = mc^2$? What does it explain?
9. What does the Doppler Effect involve? Explain its significance.
10. Define cloning.

SCIENCE

1. Benjamin Franklin.
2. These are the atomic numbers of the noble gases: helium, neon, argon, krypton, xenon and radon. Of the six, helium, neon and argon never enter into chemical compounds.
3. Louis Pasteur, who gave the world pasteurization.
4. Aluminum, which accounts for eight per cent of the earth's crust by weight.
5. Anders Celsius, an eighteenth-century Swedish astronomer.
6. Newton's Third Law of Motion.
7. Cobalt, from the German word, *kobold*, "goblin" of the mines. The ore was so named by the miners because they believed it to be worthless and "mischievous" when they were smelting and refining other metals.
8. If mass is converted to energy, the energy released (E) equals the mass (m) multiplied by the speed of light squared. This explains how enormous amounts of energy, such as atomic power, are derived from the conversion of very little mass.
9. Observation of the change in wave frequency, as of sound or light, which occurs when the source of the wave and the observer are in motion relative to one another. For example, perceived wave frequency decreases as distance increases. The observation of the Doppler Effect has been employed to determine that the universe is expanding.
10. Cloning (from the Greek *klon*, "twig") is asexual, single-parent reproduction in which offspring have the same genetic blueprint as the parent.

SCIENCE FICTION

1. Why is science fiction considered to be a separate art form from fantasy?
2. Which two European writers did the most to popularize science fiction?
3. The burning point of paper provided the title for which novel of the future?
4. Who played the part of the Bride of Frankenstein in the film of the same name?
5. Which sixteenth-century Italian poet made monsters called "orcs" famous?
6. Which science fiction author has written over 200 books on a variety of subjects?
7. The concept of "Big Brother is watching you" was devised by whom?
8. The word "robot," a mechanical man or woman, originated in which play?
9. In four film versions of Robert Louis Stevenson's novel *The Strange Case of Dr. Jekyll and Mr. Hyde*, which four actors played the lead?
10. What major science-fiction writer played a part in the development of radar and forecast the development of the satellite communication network?

SCIENCE FICTION

1. Because in science fiction the events of the story fall within the province of what is deemed future possibility.
2. Jules Verne and H.G. Wells.
3. *Fahrenheit 451*, by Ray Bradbury.
4. Valerie Hobson. (Elsa Lanchester played the bride of the creature.)
5. Ariosto.
6. Isaac Asimov.
7. George Orwell, in *1984*.
8. *R.U.R.* (Rossum's Universal Robots), by Karel Čapek.
9. John Barrymore, Frederic March, Spencer Tracy, and Jack Palance.
10. Arthur C. Clarke.

SCULPTURE

1. What sister of an emperor inspired one of Canova's most famous nude statues?

2. Who is responsible for the sculpture of the Parthenon?

3. Can you name the sculptor of the Statue of Liberty? What two objects is the figure holding?

4. A gigantic sculpture on Stone Mountain, Georgia, is a memorial to what? Whose figures are highlighted?

5. Which is the only signed figure by Michelangelo?

6. Where in Washington, D.C. is the Statue of Freedom, nicknamed Miss Freedom?

7. Which American sculptor coined a word for what has become an established art form?

8. What are the Elgin Marbles?

9. In which city would you find the celebrated statue, called "Manneken-Pis," of a little boy urinating?

10. Which modern sculptor is represented at Lincoln Center in New York by his huge "Reclining Figure" and at the National Gallery in Washington by his massive "Knife-Edge Two-Piece"?

SCULPTURE

1. Pauline Borghese, the sister of Napoleon, who was willing to pose nude because there was a fire in the room.
2. Phidias.
3. Bartholdi. In one hand is a tablet which reads "July 4, 1776," and in the other a torch held aloft. (A smaller version of the statue can be seen in Paris at the tip of an islet on the downstream side of the Pont de Grenelle over the Seine.)
4. The Confederacy. Jefferson Davis, General Robert E. Lee, and General T. J. (Stonewall) Jackson.
5. The *Pietà* in St. Peter's, in Rome.
6. On the Capitol dome.
7. Alexander Calder, whose mobiles are a type of sculpture consisting of parts that move, especially in response to air currents.
8. They are a collection of sculptures, considered to be some of the finest in the world, taken from the Parthenon in Athens in 1806 by Lord Elgin. They are now in the British Museum in London. Casts of these are in the Metropolitan Museum in New York.
9. Brussels. One story is that the statue was erected by the grateful parents of a lost little boy, whom they found in the pose depicted. Manneken-Pis is 45 centimeters (17½ inches) tall and has more than 350 costumes, which are kept at a Brussels museum, the *Maison du Roi*.
10. Henry Moore.

SEA CREATURES

1. According to the Bible, what was Jonah swallowed by? How long was he there?

2. Which fish goes through these stages of growth: fry, pan, smelt, grilse?

3. Who wrote *Moby Dick*, the story of the great white whale? What was the name of the whaling ship, and who were the captain and first mate?

4. What fish has no bony structure?

5. What mammal, closely related to the elephant, gave rise to the old mariners' tales of mermaids?

6. The term "fishwife" has come to mean a termagant, or a coarse, abusive woman. How did this arise?

7. Where would you go to catch sardines? How did they get their name?

8. Where is the valuable "sperm" of a sperm whale secreted, and for what was it formerly used?

9. What creature has a large number of blue eyes?

10. The female of what fish stores her eggs in an abdominal pouch on the male?

SEA CREATURES

1. A great fish, not a whale.
   Three days and three nights.
2. The salmon.
3. Herman Melville. *Pequod*. Ahab and Starbuck.
4. A shark, which is cartilaginous.
5. A manatee, or sea cow.
6. Billingsgate was for centuries the site of London's great fish market, and its workers were known for their loud and vulgar language. The female fish peddlers were known as "fishwives."
7. There is no such fish as a sardine. A sardine can generally contains young herring or pilchard. The word "sardine" is believed to derive from the island of Sardinia.
8. The spermaceti, a waxy substance, is located in the head of the whale and was widely used for making candles.
9. The scallop.
10. The sea horse.

SEX

1. Where do we possibly get the term "hooker"?
2. Can you give a substitute phrase for troilism?
3. In Victorian days, what was the love that dared not speak its name?
4. How does a *frotteur* get his kicks?
5. What is a catamite?
6. Explain the difference between an incubus and a succubus.
7. What does the prefix "homo-" mean in "homosexual"?
8. In which position was the French President Félix Faure when he died in 1899?
9. The biblical term "onanism" has what meaning?
10. Which well-known English author and member of Parliament wrote the following description of the female anatomy, titled "Lines on a Book Borrowed from the Ship's Doctor"?

> The portions of a woman which appeal to man's depravity
> Are constructed with considerable care,
> And what appears to you and me to be a simple cavity
> Is really quite an elaborate affair.
>
> And doctors who have bothered to examine these phenom-
> ena
> On numerous experimental dames
> Have searched the lower regions of the feminine abdomina
> And given them delightful Latin names.
>
> There's the vulva, the vagina, and the jolly perineum,
> And the hymen which is sometimes found in brides.
> And lots of other gadgets you would love if you could see
> 'em—
> The clitoris and God knows what besides.
>
> So isn't it a pity, when the common people chatter
> Of these mysteries to which I have referred,
> That they use for such a sweet and delicate a matter
> Such a very short and unattractive word?

213

SEX

1. From a section of Washington, extending south of Pennsylvania Avenue between Tenth and Fifteenth streets, which was called Hooker's Division because General Hooker's command was centered there during the Civil War. It was the vice center of Washington at the time, and Hooker's headquarters were described as "half barroom, half brothel."
2. Sex *à trois*.
3. Homosexuality.
4. By rubbing his genitalia against people in crowds.
5. A "Ganymede," a boy kept by a pederast.
6. An incubus is an evil spirit which descends upon and has sexual intercourse with a sleeping woman; a succubus is a female demon which passes under and does the same with a sleeping man.
7. "Same," from the Greek *homos*. It does not mean man.
8. He was sitting in a specially constructed sex chair with his mistress when he had a heart attack.
9. Coitus interruptus, not masturbation. (Dorothy Parker named her bird Onan because he spilled his seed upon the ground.)
10. A.P. Herbert.

SHAKESPEARE

1. Who was the Merchant of Venice?
2. In which two plays are these strange stage directions: "Enter a messenger with two heads and a hand" and "Exit pursued by a bear."?
3. Are Shakespeare's sonnets addressed to a man or a woman?
4. Who said, "She should have died hereafter," and about whom?
5. What do the following plays have in common: *A Midsummer Night's Dream, The Taming of the Shrew, Hamlet,* and *Love's Labour's Lost*?
6. Where would you find Sir Toby Belch and Sir Andrew Aguecheek?
7. What does Hamlet mean by "nunnery" when he directs Ophelia to "Get thee to a nunnery!"?
8. Who delivered the seven-ages-of-man speech, and in which play?
9. Give the alternative title of *Twelfth Night*.
10. In which play are the following words (in the original spelling) of Shakespeare to be found?

    Good friend for Jesus sake forbeare,
    To digg the dust encloased heare!
    Blest be ye man yt spares thes stones,
    And curst be he yt moves my bones.

SHAKESPEARE

1. Antonio.
2. *Titus Andronicus* and *The Winter's Tale*, respectively.
3. Both: most are addressed to a man, the last few to the famous Dark Lady of the Sonnets.
4. Macbeth, of Lady Macbeth.
5. Each contains a play within the play.
6. *Twelfth Night*.
7. It was Elizabethan slang for a whorehouse.
8. Jaques, in *As You Like It*.
9. *What You Will*.
10. In none of them. This verse is inscribed on Shakespeare's grave.

SHERLOCK HOLMES

1. Who was Arthur Conan Doyle's model for Sherlock Holmes? After whom was Holmes named?
2. "A Scandal in Bohemia" opens with "To Sherlock Holmes she is always *the* woman." Can you name her?
3. Describe "the curious incident of the dog in the night-time."
4. Where did Sir Henry Baskerville stay when the affair of *The Hound of the Baskervilles* began?
5. What connection did Sidney Paget have with the Sherlock Holmes stories?
6. What do these have in common: The Maiwand Jezails, The Trifling Monographs, The Hounds of the Baskerville (*sic*), The Crew of the Barque *Lone Star*, and The Sons of the Copper Beeches?
7. Name the American actor who wrote and starred in the play *Sherlock Holmes* early in this century. Who played Billy the pageboy in the London production in 1905?
8. At the start of which story does Dr. Watson write of a September equinoctial gale in this fashion: "As evening drew in the storm grew louder and louder, and the wind cried and sobbed like a child in the chimney."?
9. What was the title of Holmes's literary effort of his later years?
10. In whose life of Sherlock Holmes does this passage appear: "So they still live for all that love them well: in a romantic chamber of the heart, in a nostalgic country of the mind, where it is always 1895."?

SHERLOCK HOLMES

1. Joseph Bell, a consulting surgeon at the Royal Infirmary in Edinburgh, where Doyle took his medical degree. Oliver Wendell Holmes, the American physician and essayist. (Doyle took the name "Sherlock" from a cricketer he had once played against.)

2. Irene Adler.

3. In "Silver Blaze" this exchange takes place: " 'The dog did nothing in the night-time.' 'That was the curious incident,' remarked Sherlock Holmes."

4. At the Northumberland Hotel, just south of Trafalgar Square, at No. 11, Northumberland Street. The building now stands and houses the Sherlock Holmes Tavern, above which may be seen a replica of the famous rooms at 221B Baker Street.

5. Although not the first, Paget is considered the foremost illustrator of the Holmes stories. His drawings appeared in London's *Strand Magazine*, where he evolved the famous profile we know today.

6. There are groups of Sherlockian enthusiasts from various cities—respectively, Wayne, Nebraska; New Haven, Connecticut; Lombard, Illinois; Arlington, Texas; and Philadelphia, Pennsylvania.

7. Mr. William Gillette and Master Charles Chaplin (to use the form in which their names appeared in the program).

8. "The Five Orange Pips."

9. *Practical Handbook of Bee Culture with Some Observations upon the Segregation of the Queen*.

10. Vincent Starrett, in *The Private Life of Sherlock Holmes*.

SHIPS AND BOATS

1. Who said to whom: "There is *nothing*—absolutely nothing—half so much worth doing as simply messing about in boats . . . or *with* boats . . . In or out of 'em, it doesn't matter."?
2. What is the difference between a ship and a boat?
3. How many people were on Noah's ark?
4. Which was the largest passenger liner ever built?
5. What was Captain Bligh's mission when in command of the ill-fated *Bounty*? What was his rank?
6. In the following verse who was the lad "born to be king," and where is Skye?

   Speed, bonnie boat, like a bird on the wing;
      Onward, the sailors cry:
   Carry the lad that's born to be king
      Over the sea to Skye.

7. Distinguish between a sloop and a schooner.
8. The "Blue Riband," for the fastest Atlantic crossing, is held by which ship?
9. Who wrote *Two Years before the Mast*, a personal narrative which is regarded as an American classic of the days of the sailing ships?
10. For what is Sir Francis Chichester remembered?

SHIPS AND BOATS

1. Water Rat, to Mole, in *The Wind in the Willows*, by Kenneth Grahame.
2. A boat is a relatively small craft of a size that might be carried on a ship. The exception to this is the submarine, which traditionally has always been called a boat regardless of size.
3. Eight—Noah and his wife, Noah's three sons, and their wives.
4. R.M.S. *Queen Elizabeth*. This great ship came to an inglorious end when she caught fire in Hong Kong harbor after being converted into a floating university.
5. To collect breadfruit plants for replanting in the British Caribbean possessions as a source of food. At the time of the famous mutiny Bligh was a thirty-three-year-old lieutenant. He was called captain because he commanded a ship.
6. Bonnie Prince Charlie (Charles Edward Stuart, "The Young Pretender"). Skye is one of the western isles of Scotland.
7. A sloop has one fore-and-aft mast, a schooner more than one.
8. The S.S. *United States*, which averaged over 35 knots (almost 41 mph) on her maiden voyage in July 1952. It was said that she was so fireproof that only the piano and the butcher's block were of wood. Withdrawn from service in 1969, the *United States* is being refurbished for her entry into service between the West Coast and the Hawaiian Islands.
9. Richard Henry Dana.
10. Sailing alone around the world in 1966-7 in the *Gypsy Moth IV*, a 53-foot Bermuda yawl.

SOUTH AMERICA

1. Why is Brazil the only South American country to use the Portuguese language?
2. In which country is a capital not the seat of government?
3. Where are Panama hats made?
4. Who gave his name to the cold ocean current flowing north along the coasts of Chile and Peru to Ecuador?
5. For what is Portillo noted?
6. In 1894, for spying, Captain Alfred Dreyfus was deported for life to Devil's Island. Where was this infamous penal colony located?
7. A South American country and its principal river have what metal in common?
8. Which is the highest navigable lake in the world?
9. Name the two South American nations which are members of the Organization of Petroleum Exporting Countries (OPEC).
10. Where did the Marquesa de Montemayor, Uncle Pio, Pepito, Jaime, and Estaban die? Who investigated their death?

SOUTH AMERICA

1. This was arranged by a series of agreements, starting with the Treaty of Tordesillas, whereby Spain and Portugal divided the non-Christian world between them. The treaty followed a papal bull issued in 1493 by Pope Alexander VI.
2. Bolivia. Sucre, named after the first elected president of Bolivia, is the constitutional capital; La Paz is the administrative capital.
3. Ecuador.
4. Baron Alexander von Humboldt, German naturalist and explorer.
5. Located in the Chilean Andes, it is the leading ski resort in South America.
6. In the Caribbean, off French Guiana, an overseas department of France. (Dreyfus was later exonerated, and the penal colony was phased out in the 1930s.)
7. The names Argentina and Rio de la Plata both refer to silver.
8. Lake Titicaca, on the border between Peru and Bolivia.
9. Venezuela and Ecuador.
10. In the Peruvian Andes when the Bridge of San Luis Rey collapsed. In Thorton Wilder's novel, which won the Pulitzer Prize in 1927, Father Juniper, a Franciscan, investigated why they were chosen to die.

SPACE

1. In which constellation are the seven stars that form the Big Dipper?
2. What is the most abundant element in the universe?
3. Does the earth rotate on its axis from east to west or from west to east?
4. "Black holes," the first of which was discovered in 1975, are believed to be what?
5. Who wrote the words and music for "Stardust"?
6. What element was discovered in the spectrum of the sun before it was known to exist on earth?
7. Who is regarded as the father of the space age?
8. Name the only man-made structure on earth which can be identified from space.
9. Who was the first man to set foot on the moon in 1969, and what were his memorable words on the occasion?
10. How did the space shuttle *Enterprise* come by its name?

SPACE

1. *Ursa Major*, the "Great Bear," a constellation in the region of the north celestial pole, near Draco and Leo.
2. Hydrogen.
3. From west to east.
4. Superdense collapsed stars with a gravitational pull so great that not even light can escape, making them invisible. They are found by searching for evidence of extreme gravity. Scientists hope that they will tell us more about the life cycle of stars and stellar evolution.
5. Lyrics by Mitchell Parish, music by Hoagy Carmichael.
6. Helium, which is not flammable and second only to hydrogen in lightness. Its name derives from the Greek *helios*, sun.
7. Dr. Robert Goddard, who launched the first liquid-fueled rocket in 1926. It reached an altitude of 41 feet.
8. The Great Wall of China, which was built in the third century B.C. to protect China from the Nomads and winds for some 1,500 miles across Northern China.
9. Astronaut Neil Armstrong. "That's one small step for a man, one giant leap for mankind." (When this remark was first printed in the newspapers, the indefinite article "a" was missing, probably having been lost because of static in transmission from the moon. This had the effect of ruining the sense of the line, but Armstrong caught the omission, and the correct version was finally printed.)
10. It took its name from the star ship used in the TV series "Star Trek."

SPELLING TEST FOR THE LITERATE

Mark the words which are misspelled.

accidentally
accommodate
acquiesce
anoint
aquarium
assassin
battalion
beige
boundary
broccoli
calendar
caraway
cemetery
coliseum
consensus
controversy
desiccate

dittos
dyeing (coloring)
ecstasy
embarrass
frolicking
gauge
hemorrhage
hypocrisy
innovate
inoculate
judgment
kimono
liaison
liquefy
mischievous
moccasin
naphtha

parallel
paraffin
plausible
pyorrhea
queue
rarefy
sacrilegious
seize
separate
shriek
siege
sizable
supersede
ukulele
vermilion
weird
wield

SPELLING TEST
FOR THE LITERATE

They are all spelled correctly.

SPIES AND TRAITORS

1. In the Bible, who was Rahab?
2. Sir Francis Walsingham performed which important function for Elizabeth I?
3. Which well-known American married Peggy Shippen of Philadelphia, and later lived in England and Canada?
4. During the Civil War there was considerable espionage activity, but can you describe the most common type of "Northern Spy"?
5. Why is the name of Major Ferdinand Esterhazy infamous?
6. By which name was the exotic dancer Margarete Gertrude MacLeod (*née* Zelle) better known?
7. Can you identify George Smiley?
8. Who was Cicero?
9. Where in New York was the house depicted in the film *The House on 92nd Street*, about Nazi espionage?
10. Which famous spy is buried in Westminster Abbey in London?

SPIES AND TRAITORS

1. The harlot who lodged the two men sent by Joshua to spy "the land, even Jericho." (Joshua 2:1).
2. He developed an efficient political spy system for her.
3. Benedict Arnold, who had arranged to betray West Point in return for money and a British commission. In exile after the Revolution, he lived in Canada and England, where he was generally spurned.
4. It is a large late-ripening, yellowish-red apple.
5. Esterhazy was a principal in the Dreyfus Affair in France, during which Captain Alfred Dreyfus was convicted of treason and deported to Devil's Island for life. Esterhazy was the real traitor, who gave to the German military attaché in Paris the *bordereau* (schedule) listing secret French documents.
6. Mata Hari. Dutch-born, she worked as a German spy in World War I, extracting military secrets from high Allied officers who were intimate with her. In 1917 she was arrested and executed by the French. Her stage name Mata Hari means Eye of the Morning in Javanese.
7. He was the leading character in the novel *The Spy Who Came in from the Cold*, by John Le Carré.
8. It was the code name for the German agent who served as valet to the British Ambassador to Turkey in World War II and photographed many top-secret Allied documents.
9. On East Ninety-third Street, between Park and Madison Avenues. It was later demolished.
10. Major John André, the British agent in the American Revolution, who negotiated with Benedict Arnold for the betrayal of West Point.

SPORT

1. What is the most heavily attended spectator sport in the United States?
2. In rodeo competition, what is the standard required time for a rider to stay on in bareback, saddle bronc, and bull-riding events?
3. What are the Bugaboos and why are they famous?
4. Canada and Scotland regularly play for the Strathcona Cup in what sport?
5. What popular sport was invented by James Naismith, a Y.M.C.A. college instructor?
6. In which sport are "sculls" and "sweeps" used, and what is the difference?
7. What is the more familiar name of Edson Arantes do Nascimento?
8. What is the distance of the marathon race and why?
9. "Walking the dog," "tick-tack," and "tie hop" are terms used in which activity?
10. In *A Woman of No Importance*, how does Oscar Wilde describe the English country gentleman galloping after a fox?

SPORT

1. Horse racing.
2. Eight seconds.
3. They are mountains in British Columbia which are considered to offer the most challenging and dangerous skiing terrain in the world. The skiing areas of deep powder snow can only be reached by helicopter from a base camp.
4. Curling—a game like bowls, played on ice, in which two teams slide heavy oblate stones toward a target circle at either end.
5. Basketball. He invented it to fill the seasonal gap between football in the autumn and baseball in the spring.
6. Rowing. In a scull each rower has two oars, each about 9 feet long. Sculls can be "singles," "doubles," "quads," or "octopedes." In a sweep each rower has a 12-foot oar. Sweeps come in "pairs," "fours," and "eights."
7. Pelé, the famous Brazilian soccer player.
8. In 490 B.C. the Athenian army, outnumbered ten to one, defeated 100,000 Persians at the Battle of Marathon. A runner, Pheidippides, brought the news to Athens, which lay some 25 miles away. When the Olympic Games were revived in 1896, a race covering approximately the same distance was included in the events. In 1908, when the Olympics were held in London, the race started at Windsor Castle and ended at London's White City, a distance of 26 miles. King Edward VII, insisted that the race finish in front of the Royal Box, which increased the length to 26 miles, 385 yards. This is now the standard distance.
9. Skateboarding.
10. "The unspeakable in full pursuit of the uneatable."

STRANGE PRACTICES

1. Can you describe the strange practice known as suttee?
2. The body of which deceased world leader is on daily exhibition?
3. What is a trigamist?
4. Vlad IV, a fifteenth-century prince of Wallachia, was called Vlad the Impaler because of his penchant for impaling his prisoners on wooden stakes when they were still alive. By which name, more familiar in another context, was he also known?
5. In Robert Service's poem, what was the strange thing done "that night on the marge of Lake Lebarge"?
6. What has occurred in the worship of Juggernaut, whose statue is mounted on an enormous temple cart and dragged by pilgrims in an annual rite?
7. According to the French, what is *le vice anglais*?
8. Define purdah.
9. What is meant by defenestration?
10. Why is the sexual life of the camel stranger than anyone thinks, according to an anonymous source?

STRANGE PRACTICES

1. The act, now forbidden by law, of a Hindu widow cremating herself on her husband's funeral pyre.
2. Lenin, whose embalmed remains may be seen in a transparent casket in a mausoleum outside the Kremlin walls in Moscow.
3. A man with three wives, or a woman with three husbands.
4. Dracula. He was the son of Vlad Dracul (Vlad the Devil) and was called Dracula, or Son of the Devil. Bram Stoker took this name for the title of his famous novel about vampires.
5. "The Cremation of Sam McGee."
6. Worshipers are said to have thrown themselves under the immense wheels of the wagon to be crushed to death.
7. Flagellation.
8. It is the Hindu practice of secluding women from men or strangers.
9. An act of throwing someone or something out of a window (Latin *fenestra*, window).
10.
        The sexual life of the camel
            Is stranger than anyone thinks,
        For when his obsessions obsess him,
            A beeline he makes for the Sphinx.
        Now the Sphinx's exterior orifice
            Is buried in the sands of the Nile,
        Which accounts for the hump on the camel,
            And the Sphinx's inscrutable smile.

TELEVISION

1. Who invented television?
2. When and where did the first successful broadcast occur?
3. Who once referred to television as "a vast wasteland?"
4. What was the longest-running western in television history?
5. Which company is the most successful producer of TV game shows?
6. Give the occupations of Ralph Kramden (Jackie Gleason) and Ed Norton (Art Carney) in "The Honeymooners."
7. The "Masterpiece Theatre" programs that appear on PBS (public broadcasting service stations) are underwritten by a grant from which corporation?
8. Name the longest-running TV series in this country.
9. Who is television's most highly paid performer?
10. What new concept in TV dramatic programming resulted in the largest viewing audience in history?

TELEVISION

1. No one. The "invention" of television was not one single act, but a series of independent yet interlocking discoveries.
2. In 1936, in London, when there were about 100 sets in the whole United Kingdom.
3. Newton Minow, when Chairman of the Federal Communications Commission.
4. "Gunsmoke," which ran for just under 20 years.
5. Goodson-Todman Productions, which has been responsible for such shows as "I've Got a Secret," "To Tell the Truth," and "What's My Line?"
6. Bus driver and sewer worker, or self-styled sanitation engineer.
7. Mobil Corporation.
8. "Meet the Press," which is devoted to interviews with contemporary political and social figures, has been running since 1947.
9. Johnny Carson, the host of the "Tonight" show. His current five-year NBC contract reputedly calls for annual payments of $2,500,000 plus a percentage of commercial fees.
10. The miniseries "Roots," in 1976, on ABC with an estimated viewing audience of 130 million people.

THE THEATRE

1. Name the four most important Greek dramatists. Which one is the exception to the others?

2. With what two celebrated actresses did Bernard Shaw carry on famous correspondences?

3. Who slept in a coffin and played a most unusual Hamlet?

4. What was the title of the play Lincoln was watching at Ford's Theatre the night he was shot?

5. "Experience is the name everyone gives to their mistakes" is a typical line from a nineteenth-century drawing-room comedy by what author?

6. How did Vladimir and Estragon pass their time, only to be disappointed in the end?

7. Can you name the famous actress whose youthful beauty attracted so many royal protectors that she was called "the sport of kings"?

8. What is the name of the Broadway theater award, and for whom is it named?

9. *Oh! Calcutta!* is a play on what French words?

10. Which musicals featured the following songs? Who were the composers and lyricists?

    a) "I Hate Men"
    b) "Mack the Knife"
    c) "Get Me to the Church on Time"
    d) "It Ain't Necessarily So"
    e) "Diamonds Are a Girl's Best Friend"

THE THEATRE

1. Aeschylus, Aristophanes, Euripides, Sophocles. Aristophanes wrote comedies, the others tragedies.
2. Ellen Terry and Mrs. Patrick Campbell.
3. Sarah Bernhardt. When she played Hamlet, she had one leg.
4. *Our American Cousin*, a comedy of Yankee life, by the English dramatist Tom Taylor.
5. Oscar Wilde, in *Lady Windemere's Fan*.
6. Waiting for Godat, who never appeared, in Samuel Beckett's play.
7. Lillie Langtry, who was known as the Jersey Lily after the island where she was born.
8. The Tony, in honor of Antoinette Perry, the founder of the American Theater Wing.
9. *"O! Quelle cul tu as!"* (Oh, What an ass you have!)
10. a) *Kiss Me Kate*, by Cole Porter
    b) *Threepenny Opera*, by Marc Blitzstein and Kurt Weill
    c) *My Fair Lady*, by Alan Jay Lerner and Frederick Loewe
    d) *Porgy and Bess*, by Ira Gershwin and George Gershwin
    e) *Gentlemen Prefer Blondes*, by Leo Robin and Jule Styne

THREE OF A KIND

1. What were the names of Noah's three sons?
2. What does the phrase "lock, stock, and barrel" signify, and to what does it refer?
3. Who had as their motto "All for one, one for all"? What were their names?
4. Who sailed off one night in a wooden shoe?
5. Name the three rulers who met in 1872 to form the informal alliance called the Three Emperors' League.
6. Can you identify Huey, Dewey, and Louie?
7. What is the name of the Russian sled that is drawn by three horses abreast?
8. What three civil servants were greatly burned up by the king but were later promoted?
9. Rub-a-dub-dub
   Three men in a tub,
   And who do you think they be?
10. Who were Julius, Leonard, and Adolph better known as?

THREE OF A KIND

1. Shem, Ham, and Japheth.
2. The whole of anything—the lock, or firing mechanism stock, and barrel being the basic parts of a firearm.
3. The Three Musketeers, from the novel of the same name by Alexandre Dumas, père, were Athos, Porthos, and Aramis.
4. Winken, Blynken, and Nod "Sailed on a river of crystal light / Into a sea of dew," according to the poem by Eugene Field.
5. The Emperors Franz Josef of Austria, Wilhelm I of Germany, and Alexander II of Russia.
6. They are Donald Duck's nephews.
7. A troika.
8. Shadrach, Meshach, and Abednego were cast "into the midst of a burning fiery furnace" because they would not worship the golden idol built by Nebuchadnezzar, King of Babylon. They were saved by the intervention of an angel of the Lord (Daniel 3: 13-30).
9. "The butcher, the baker, the candlestick-maker."
10. The Marx Brothers—Groucho, Chico, and Harpo.

TIME AND TIDE

1. On what is time calculated throughout the world?
2. Is a neap tide the least or the greatest tide in a lunar month?
3. Who wrote the following epigram?

   I am a sundial, and I make a botch
   Of what is done far better by a watch.

4. The hands of clocks or watches in advertisements are generally set at what time?
5. Where would you go to find "Big Ben," and how would you describe it?
6. What, did the Walrus say, has come?
7. A *tsunami* is usually, although inexactly, known as what?
8. Who declared, in a ringing pamphlet, that "These are the times that try men's souls."?
9. Where are the highest tides in the world?
10. Can you name the author of the following lines?

    The blood-dimmed tide is loosed, and everywhere
    The ceremony of innocence is drowned;
    The best lack all conviction, while the worst
    Are full of passionate intensity.

TIME AND TIDE

1. On the basis of Greenwich mean time, which is the mean solar time for the prime meridian (0°) at the Royal Observatory at Greenwich, England.
2. The least.
3. Hilaire Belloc, *Sonnets and Verse*.
4. Approximately ten past ten, presumably for the sake of symmetry and to frame the manufacturer's name. Eighteen minutes to four is also used if an advertising message is printed over the upper half of the dial.
5. London. "Big Ben" is not the tower, nor is it the clock. It is the huge bell that strikes the hour. It was named for Sir Benjamin Hall, who was the first Commissioner of Works when it was installed.
6.   "The time has come," the Walrus said,
        "To talk of many things:
    Of shoes—and ships—and sealing-wax—
        Of cabbages—and kings—
    And why the sea is boiling hot—
        And whether pigs have wings."
            —*Through the Looking-Glass*, by Lewis Carroll
7. A tidal wave. *Tsunami* is the Japanese word for "harbor wave." These waves, which cause enormous devastation when they reach land, are generally caused by submarine earthquake or volcanic eruption.
8. Thomas Paine, in *Common Sense*, published in 1776.
9. The Bay of Fundy, in eastern Canada, where the sea level changes by 40 feet during the day.
10. William Butler Yeats, "The Second Coming."

TITLES

Give the quotation from which the following titles are taken, naming also the work and the author.

1. *Gone with the Wind*, by Margaret Mitchell
2. *The Grapes of Wrath*, by John Steinbeck
3. *The Little Foxes*, by Lillian Hellman
4. *Remembrance of Things Past (À la recherche du temps perdu)*, by Marcel Proust
5. *My Fair Lady*, by Alan Jay Lerner and Frederick Loewe
6. *Eyeless in Gaza*, by Aldous Huxley
7. *Cakes and Ale*, by W. Somerset Maugham
8. *The Voice of the Turtle*, by John van Druten
9. *Far from the Madding Crowd*, by Thomas Hardy
10. *Arms and the Man*, by George Bernard Shaw

TITLES

1. "I have forgot much, Cynara! gone with the wind,
   Flung roses, roses riotously with the throng."
   —"Non Sum Qualis Eram Bonae Sub Regno Cynarae," by Ernest Dowson

2. "Mine eyes have seen the glory of the coming of the Lord;
   He is trampling out the vintage where the grapes of wrath are stored."
   —"Battle Hymn of the Republic," by Julia Ward Howe

3. "The little foxes, that spoil the vines"
   —Song of Solomon 2:15

4. "When to the sessions of sweet silent thought
   I summon up remembrance of things past"
   —Sonnet No. 30, by Shakespeare

5. "London Bridge is broken down,
   My fair lady."
   —"London Bridge" (Anonymous)

6. "Eyeless in Gaza, at the Mill with slaves"
   —"Samson Agonistes" by John Milton

7. "Dost thou think, because thou art virtuous, there shall be no more cakes and ale?"
   —Shakespeare's *Twelfth Night*, Act II, Scene 3

8. "The flowers appear on the earth; the time of the singing of birds is come, and the voice of the turtle is heard in our land."
   —Song of Solomon 2:12

9. "Far from the madding crowd's ignoble strife,
   Their sober wishes never learned to stray."
   —"Elegy Written in a Country Churchyard" by Thomas Gray

10. "Arms and the man I sing" (*Arma virumque cano*)
    —*Aeneid*, by Virgil

TRANSPORTATION

1. What is the function of the mules used at the Panama Canal?
2. An automobile bearing the initials CH comes from what country?
3. A Nantucket sleigh-ride refers to what?
4. Who made the first successful nonstop flight across the Atlantic Ocean? When?
5. What significant event occurred at Promontory Point, Utah, in 1869?
6. What might the Chunnel be?
7. Of what words is taxicab the shortened form?
8. To whom is the command "Mush!" given, and what is the derivation of the term?
9. Why was the first Duke of Wellington opposed to the newly emerging railroads in Great Britain?
10. On what track would you find the Chattanooga Choo-Choo?

TRANSPORTATION

1. Mules are the small electric locomotives used to pull ships through the locks.
2. Switzerland. CH is the abbreviation for the country's formal Latin name, *Confederatio Helvetica*, The Swiss Confederation.
3. A ride in a whaleboat behind a harpooned whale.
4. John W. Alcock and Arthur W. Brown, in 1919, from Newfoundland to Ireland.
5. The completion of the first U.S. transcontinental railroad, when the Union Pacific Railroad coming from Nebraska met the Central Pacific from California. They drove a golden spike to celebrate the occasion.
6. A proposed tunnel under the English Channel.
7. Taximeter-cabriolet. Taxi is from the French *taxe*, charge, and cabriolet is derived from the Latin *caper*, meaning he-goat, in allusion to the taxi's bounding motion.
8. To a team of sled dogs, to start or go faster. It is derived from the Canadian French *mouche*!, fly!
9. "Because they would encourage the lower orders to move about."
10. Track 29.

TRAVELS AND VOYAGES

1. Which expedition leader first succeeded in circumnavigating the earth in one voyage?
2. Who traveled with Charley?
3. Can you give a popular derivation of the word "posh" that arises from a luxurious type of accommodation on a long sea voyage?
4. What widely-traveled Venetian brought pasta to Italy?
5. What young Cambridge graduate sailed around the world on board the ten-gun brig H.M.S. *Beagle*?
6. Who was the avaricious old boatman who ferried the unfortunate ones across a river?
7. "I met a traveler from an antique land . . ." is the beginning of what famous poem?
8. What was the name of the surgeon who sailed from England on a series of voyages, starting with the merchant ship *Antelope* in 1699? In the course of his travels he encountered all sorts of people, including some mad scientists trying to extract sunshine from cucumbers. He returned to England with a great admiration for horses.
9. How was the Reform Club at 104/5 Pall Mall, London, connected with a celebrated trip?
10. Who went around the world in 72 days in 1890?

TRAVELS AND VOYAGES

1. Not Ferdinand Magellan, but Sir Francis Drake, in a voyage lasting just under three years, from 1577 to 1580. Magellan sailed halfway around on two separate voyages. He was killed by natives in the Philippines on his second voyage, but the expedition continued under Juan Sebastián del Cano, who became the first man to circumnavigate the globe in 1522.

2. John Steinbeck, in his book *Travels With Charley: In Search of America* (with his dog, a French poodle.)

3. It is said that in the days of the British raj, well-heeled passengers on a round trip to India requested choice cabins on the shady side of the ship—that is, "port out, starboard home," giving us the acronym "posh." This, however, must come under the heading of folk etymology as there is no firm evidence that it is true. The Oxford English Dictionary states that the derivation of the word is obscure.

4. Marco Polo, after his extensive travels in China in the thirteenth century. Besides pasta he told of asbestos, coal, paper currency, and other phenomena virtually unknown in Europe.

5. Charles Darwin, who held the post of naturalist on the ship. It was on this voyage that he visited the Galapagos Islands, where he found among the exotic flora and fauna key evidence for his theory of evolution.

6. Charon, who ferried the dead across the Styx, one of the five rivers separating Hades from the land of the living. According to Greek mythology, the passenger paid with the coin left in his mouth when he was buried.

7. "Ozymandias," by Percy Bysshe Shelley.

8. Lemuel Gulliver, the hero of Jonathan Swift's satiric masterpiece *Gulliver's Travels*.

9. In Jules Verne's story *Around the World in Eighty Days*, it was there that Phileas Fogg began and ended his fabulous trip, and won his wager.

10. Nelly Bly, the pseudonym of an enterprising New York journalist named Elizabeth C. Seaman, who wanted to rival the feat accomplished by the fictional Phileas Fogg.

THE UNITED STATES

1. Which state was named after Queen Elizabeth?
2. What was an early name, and still is the official name, of Rhode Island?
3. How did Manhattan Island in New York City get its name?
4. Which state is named after an English lord?
5. Name the easternmost state that extends further south than the northernmost boundary of Virginia and further north than the southernmost boundary of Rhode Island.
6. Which four states meet at Four Corners?
7. Where is the rainiest spot in the United States?
8. Name seven of the ten states east of the Mississippi whose names have Indian roots. This excludes Minnesota, which is divided by this river, and Indiana, which is derived from our word for the red man.
9. Which large U.S. city was so named by its pious founder because it reminded him of an old city in Asia Minor that was faithful to Christianity?
10. Can you name the southernmost, northernmost, easternmost, and westernmost states?

THE UNITED STATES

1. Virginia, after the Virgin Queen.
2. Rhode Island and Providence Plantations. The longest name belongs to the smallest state.
3. When Pieter Minuit gave the equivalent of $24 in trinkets for the island, he dealt with an Indian tribe that called itself Manna-hata or Manahatin. They were in fact the Carnasies, who held no right to the island, and Minuit had to pay the real Manna-hatas later. It was still a good buy.
4. Delaware, in honor of Lord de la Warr, who was briefly governor of Virginia. The name was first applied to a bay, then a river, and finally a state.
5. New Jersey.
6. Arizona, Colorado, New Mexico, and Utah.
7. On Mt. Waialeale on the island of Kauai in Hawaii, it rains for 350 days during the year.
8. Alabama, Connecticut, Illinois, Kentucky, Massachusetts, Michigan, Mississippi, Ohio, Tennessee, and Wisconsin.
9. Philadelphia, founded by William Penn. Its Greek roots mean "brotherly love."
10. Hawaii is the most southern, and Alaska is the correct answer for the other three categories. It is the most eastern because the 180° longitude line, which separates the hemispheres, lies just to the east of the Aleutian Islands of Attu, Kiska, and Amchitka.

U.S. PRESIDENTS

1. Who was the first president to occupy the White House?
2. Can you name the first man to be defeated in a presidential election?
3. Who was the youngest president?
4. Who is Leslie Lynch King, Jr.?
5. Who was the first president to have been born in a hospital?
6. After leaving the presidency, what did John Adams and Thomas Jefferson have in common?
7. Can you name the person who is a grandchild of one president and the great grandchild of another?
8. What did Grover Cleveland do at the White House that no other president did there?
9. Lincoln never did it, Theodore Roosevelt did it 37 times, Richard Nixon is trying it three times. What is it?
10. Who made the astute observation that "when more and more people are thrown out of work, unemployment results?"

U.S. PRESIDENTS

1. John Adams, in 1800.
2. Thomas Jefferson, when he lost to John Adams in 1796. (George Washington was unopposed in previous elections.)
3. When Theodore Roosevelt became president on September 14, 1901, on McKinley's death, he was within forty-three days of his forty-third birthday. (John F. Kennedy was the youngest elected president, at the age of forty-three.)
4. Gerald R. Ford, the thirty-eighth president. His parents were divorced when he was two, and when his mother remarried, he assumed the name of his stepfather.
5. Jimmy Carter.
6. They both died on the same day, July 4, 1826.
7. Jennie Eisenhower, the daughter of Julie Nixon Eisenhower and David Eisenhower.
8. He was married there to Frances Folsom.
9. Writing a book.
10. Calvin Coolidge.

WAR

1. Who said, "There never was a good war or a bad peace"?
2. Which colonel under British jurisdiction surrendered to the French at Fort Necessity in 1754 during the French and Indian War?
3. Which battle is said to have been won on the playing fields of Eton?
4. To what was Maréchal Bosquet referring when he observed: *"C'est magnifique, mais ce n'est pas la guerre."* (It's magnificent, but it isn't war.)?
5. What is shrapnel, and how did it get its name?
6. What was a sutler's function in the armies of the past?
7. How did the term "fifth column," for secret subversives working within a country, come about?
8. Who were referred to as "the Ladies from Hell"?
9. How many Generals of the Armies has the U.S. had?
10. Which war lasted the longest—the War of American Independence, the Civil War, or World War II?

WAR

1. Benjamin Franklin, in a letter to Josiah Quincy, September 11, 1773.

2. George Washington.

3. Waterloo. There is no firm evidence, however, that Wellington ever said this.

4. The gallant but foolhardy Charge of the Light Brigade during the Battle of Balaclava in the Crimean War, October 1854. (When oleomargarine was introduced as a substitute for butter in England in 1914, *Punch* magazine commented: *"C'est magnifique, mais ce n'est pas la beurre."*)

5. An anti-personnel projectile containing metal balls, fused to explode in the air above enemy troops, or the metal balls in such a projectile. It was invented by Lieutenant (later General) Henry Shrapnel, a British artillery officer. Shrapnel should not be confused with shell fragments.

6. A camp follower who peddled provisions to the soldiers.

7. During the Spanish Civil War the general attacking Madrid said he was in charge of five columns: four advancing from the outside and "the fifth column within the city." Ernest Hemingway popularized the phrase by using it as the title of a play.

8. The kilted Highland regiments of World War I, who went into battle to the death-defying skirl of the pipes.

9. One—General John J. Pershing, commander in chief of the American Expeditionary Force in World War I. Five-star generals in World War II were called Generals of the Army.

10. The War Of American Indepence (1775-1783).

WATER

1. Name the principal oceans of the world.
2. Which famous French revolutionary was murdered in his bath by whom?
3. Which is the largest lake in the world?
4. Name the author of *The Cruel Sea*.
5. Who wrote the following, and what was the name of the work?

   I must go down to the seas again, to the lonely sea and the sky.

6. Who was surprised in her bath by a pair of lascivious elders who made indecent proposals to her and later lied to cover up their guilt?
7. Locate and describe the Sargasso Sea.
8. Why is New York City's East River geographically misnamed?
9. Who, when bathing, cried "Eureka!" because he had discovered an important principle of physics? What was the principle involved, and what does "Eureka" mean?
10. Who says the following?

    I chatter, chatter as I flow
       To join the brimming river,
    For men may come and men may go,
       But I go on for ever.

    What institution takes its name from this?

WATER

1. The Atlantic, Pacific, Indian, their southern extensions in Antarctica, and the Arctic.
2. Jean Paul Marat, by Charlotte Corday in 1793. While hiding in the sewers of Paris, Marat contracted a skin disease which required treatments in a warm bath.
3. The Caspian Sea is the largest inland sea or lake in the world, with an area of about 144,000 square miles. The fresh-water lake with the greatest surface area, about 31,800 square miles, is Lake Superior, one of the Great Lakes.
4. Nicholas Monsarrat.
5. John Masefield, "Sea-Fever."
6. Susannah, as related in the book of Daniel, from the Apocrypha. The falsity of the elders was subsequently exposed by sharp cross-questioning by Daniel, and they were duly punished. (Apocrypha, Daniel 13)
7. It is a section of the North Atlantic Ocean between the West Indies and the Azores. It is a relatively still area, with an abundance of seaweed in the center of a great swirl of ocean currents.
8. The East River is not a river but a strait, or connecting body of water, between the Harlem River (which is not a river either) and Long Island Sound on the north and the Atlantic Ocean on the south.
9. Archimedes, a Greek mathematician, physicist, and inventor, observing the overflow of water in his bath, discovered the principle, known today by his name, that the volume of an irregular solid can be measured by the displacement of water. "Eureka" (Greek *heureka*) means "I have found (it)."
10. The Brook, in the poem of the same name by Alfred, Lord Tennyson. The Brook, a men's club in New York.

WEATHER

1. Who is reputed to have said, "Everybody talks about the weather, but nobody does anything about it."?
2. In classical mythology, who was controller of the winds?
3. What was the chief characteristic of the Pleistocene Epoch?
4. Who inquired, "Where are the snows of yesteryear?"?
5. Define isobars.
6. Can you complete the couplet beginning, "Red sky at night . . ."?
7. How does the Gulf Stream affect the climate?
8. To what was Shelley referring in these lines?

   > I am the daughter of Earth and Water,
   >   And the nursling of the Sky;
   > I pass through the pores of the oceans and shores,
   >   I change, but I cannot die.

9. What does the Beaufort Scale measure?
10. There is a famous inscription from Herodotus on the front of the Main Post Office in New York City that has often been parodied. Can you recall the words?

WEATHER

1. It has been attributed to Mark Twain, although the line is not found in his published works. It does, however, appear in the editorial column of the Hartford *Courant,* written by his friend Charles Dudley Warner.
2. Aeolus.
3. The alternate appearance and recession of northern glaciation, also called the Ice Age.
4. François Villon, in *"Ballade des Dames du Temps Jadis"*.
5. They are lines on a map connecting points of equal barometric pressure.
6. Red sky at night, sailors delight—
   Red sky at morning, sailors take warning.
7. Its warming waters raise the average temperature of areas in the higher latitudes.
8. A cloud.
9. The Beaufort Scale, devised by Admiral Beaufort of the Royal Navy, is a scale by which successive ranges of wind velocities are assigned numbers. An adaptation of it, used by the U.S. Weather Service, employs numbers from 0 to 12, representing wind velocities from calm to hurricane.
10. "Neither snow, nor rain, nor heat, nor gloom of night stays these couriers from the swift completion of their appointed rounds."

WEIGHTS AND MEASURES

1. What unit of measurement is used to measure the height of a horse?
2. Explain why "lb." is the abbreviation for pound.
3. On a thermometer when are the Fahrenheit and centigrade readings identical?
4. Do you know the derivation of the word "ton"? What is the difference between a short, or regular, ton and a long ton?
5. In the metric system, approximately what does one liter of water weigh?
6. A cubit is an ancient unit of linear measurement mentioned often in the Bible. In what fashion was it determined?
7. In cooking, how many drops make a dash? How many pinches to a teaspoon?
8. What is the capacity of a ten-gallon hat?
9. How is one's weight measured in Great Britain?
10. Can you name the dark comedy by Shakespeare that was set in Vienna?

WEIGHTS AND MEASURES

1. A hand, equal to four inches.
2. From the Latin *libra*, "scales"—hence "pound."
3. At −40°
4. It derives from the Old English *tunne*, meaning a cask or measure of wine. A short ton is 2,000 pounds and a long ton 2,240 pounds.
5. One kilogram, which is about 2.2 pounds.
6. Originally it was the length of the forearm from the tip of the middle finger to the elbow, or about 17–22 inches.
7. Six drops. Eight pinches.
8. Less than a gallon.
9. The standard unit of human weight in Britain is the stone, which is equivalent to 14 pounds.
10. *Measure for Measure*.

WHO SAID IT FIRST?

1. "If a house be divided against itself, that house cannot stand."
2. "*L'état c'est moi.*" (I am the state.)
3. "Survival of the fittest."
4. "*Qu'ils mangent de la brioche.*" (Let them eat cake.)
5. "Make a better mousetrap and the world will beat a path to your door."
6. "Nothing is so much to be feared as fear."
7. "Murder will out."
8. "Iron Curtain."
9. "It is now the moment to recall what our country has done for each of us, and to ask ourselves what we can do for our country in return."
10. "Any man who hates dogs and babies can't be all bad."

WHO SAID IT FIRST?

1. The Bible: Mark 3:25. Lincoln used this quotation, slightly changed, in an 1858 speech.
2. Although commonly attributed to Louis XIV, there is no firm evidence to prove that he said it. Napoleon, however, did—in a speech to the French senate in 1814.
3. Herbert Spencer, although Charles Darwin later adopted it.
4. Certainly not Marie Antoinette. It appears in Rousseau's *Confessions* written before she even arrived in France.
5. Emerson wrote in his *Journal*: "better chairs or knives, crucibles, or church organs" but never alluded to mousetraps.
6. Thoreau, in his *Journal* of 1851. Franklin D. Roosevelt may have unconsciously borrowed this thought when he declared in his first inaugural address, "The only thing we have to fear is fear itself."
7. Geoffrey Chaucer in *The Canterbury Tales*. In *Hamlet* (Act II, Scene I), Shakespeare wrote: "For murder though it have no tongue will speak . . ."
8. H.G. Wells, in his science-fiction novel *The Food of the Gods*, published in 1904. The phrase was also employed by Goebbels, Hitler's minister of Propaganda, during World War II. Churchill again popularized the term in his speech at Westminster College, Fulton, Missouri, in 1946, when he said, "From Stettin in the Baltic to Trieste in the Adriatic an iron curtain has descended across the Continent."
9. Oliver Wendell Holmes, Jr., in an address given in 1884. Warren G. Harding also expressed the same thought, which, however, is best remembered from John F. Kennedy's inaugural address: ". . . Ask not what your country can do for you; ask what you can do for your country."
10. It was not said by W.C. Fields, but about him, by Leo Rosten, at a dinner for Fields in 1939. (*Bartlett's Familiar Quotations* mistakenly attributes the line to Fields.)

THE WILD WEST

1. Who authorized negotiations for the Louisiana Purchase in 1803?
2. In which state is the Donner Pass, and for what is it known?
3. Who was engaged in the shoot-out in 1881 at the O.K. Corral in Tombstone, Arizona?
4. Can you describe a Buntline Special?
5. Why are John Sutter and his mill famous?
6. The fringe on buckskin shirts and jackets served what effective purpose?
7. How many acres of unoccupied public land were granted to a settler under the Homestead Act of 1862?
8. Can you give the origin of the word "cowpoke"?
9. In the fur trade, what were "hairy bank notes"?
10. What was the name of the notorious character who is reputed to have had 12 husbands, who dressed, cursed and shot like a man, and who was buried beside Wild Bill Hickock in Deadwood, South Dakota?

THE WILD WEST

1. President Thomas Jefferson.
2. California, high up in the Sierra Nevada. It was there that a group of 87 emigrants, including two Donner families, were trapped in the snow during the winter of 1846-47. Only half survived, and the remaining members were driven to cannibalism.
3. The Earps (Wyatt and his brothers, Morgan and Virgil) and Doc Holliday versus the Clanton and McLaury brothers.
4. It is a long-barreled, 12-inch variant of the two most popular pistols of the West: the .44 and .45 Colt single-action revolvers. Novelist Ned Buntline gave these to Wyatt Earp, Bat Masterson, and others.
5. It was the discovery of gold at Sutter's Mill that started the California gold rush.
6. It helped to shed the rainwater.
7. The Act provided for the transfer of a quarter square mile section of 160 acres to each homesteader on payment of a nominal fee after five years of residence.
8. One of his duties was to poke the cattle in the boxcars to keep them on their feet so that the car could be filled to capacity on its way to the market. Of course, he also poked or punched cattle to keep them moving on the range.
9. Beaver pelts, just as a buck, short for the buckskin used in trade, has come to mean a dollar.
10. Martha Jane Canary, otherwise known as Calamity Jane.

WINE

1. Is Chablis a red or white wine? A Bordeaux or a Burgundy?
2. In France the *Appellation d'Origine Contrôlée* (A.O.C.) laws regulate the production of what?
3. The names of most Alsatian wines contain what sort of information?
4. The indentation on the bottom of some wine bottles, which is called a kick or a punt, serves what two purposes?
5. Which grape makes the most successful white wine of California?
6. Name the two South American countries which produce good to excellent wines that are relatively inexpensive.
7. Which city in Spain lends its name to the fortified wine known as sherry?
8. The finest Chianti "Classico," which may carry the symbol of the Black Rooster on the label, is produced where in Italy?
9. Who drew the famous *New Yorker* cartoon of a host at a dinner party proudly explaining to his guests, "It's a naive domestic Burgundy without any breeding, but I think you'll be amused by its presumption."?
10. Champagne comes in a wide selection of sizes. Can you name eight of the ten bottle sizes and the amount of wine in each?

263

WINE

1. Chablis is a white Burgundy. It is also a generic name for bulk wine in many other, non-European parts of the world, including the United States and Canada.
2. Only the premier wines of France.
3. The grape variety from which they are made, such as Riesling or Sylvaner, rather than a vineyard or village.
4. To strengthen the bottle and to catch sediment in the wine.
5. Chardonnay, called Pinot Chardonnay in France.
6. Argentina and Chile.
7. Jerez de la Frontera. The wine was formerly pronounced "sherris" from Xeres, the older name of Jerez, dating from the Moorish conquest.
8. In a specific geographical district located between Florence and Siena.
9. James Thurber.
10. Usually available are

1) Nip or split	¼ bottle
2) Half bottle	½ bottle
3) Quart	1 bottle
4) Magnum	2 bottles
5) Jeroboam	4 bottles

After the jeroboam come the curiosities. Because of their size, it is not practical to produce champagne in them, and they are generally filled from a number of smaller bottles.

6) Rehoboam	6 bottles
7) Methuselah	8 bottles
8) Salmanazar	12 bottles
9) Balthazar	16 bottles
10) Nebuchadnezzar	20 bottles

WOMEN

1. Who was the first prominent American advocate of women's rights?
2. What female American Indian was a huge social success in London?
3. To be a quean was to be what in sixteenth and seventeenth-century Britain?
4. Who was married to two kings and was the dominant figure in the politics, culture, and social life of twelfth-century Europe?
5. What is a "Messalina"?
6. What was the original meaning of a gossip?
7. What popular, muckraking magazine is named for an American labor organizer?
8. Who was Dulcinea?
9. What etymological connection does the word lady have with bread?
10. In June 1893, a brutal double ax-murder in Fall River, Massachusetts, inspired the following bit of doggerel:

   > Lizzie Borden took an ax
   > And gave her mother forty whacks;
   > When she saw what she had done
   > She gave her father forty-one.

   What was the verdict in the trial of Lizzie Borden?

WOMEN

1. Abigail Adams, the wife of future President John Adams, because she asked in vain that women's rights be included in the Constitution.
2. Pocahontas.
3. A bold or ill-behaved woman; a jade; a strumpet.
4. Eleanor of Aquitaine. She was married to Louis VII of France and Henry II of England.
5. An oversexed woman. Messalina was the third wife of the Roman Emperor Claudius I.
6. Among the early English, a *godsibb* was a sponsor at a baptism, the *god* part of the word standing for God, and *sibb* meaning Kinsman. The word later came to mean a "boon companion" and then gossip as we know the term.
7. *Mother Jones*. Her real name was Mary Harris Jones (1830-1930)
8. The imaginary love of Don Quixote.
9. In Anglo-Saxon times the most important duty of the housewife was the making of bread, and she was called a *Llaefidge*, or bread-kneader, which subsequently evolved into lady. In the 1600's, however, the word fell into disrepute, and to be a lady was largely to be a lady of pleasure. Now it has come into its own again as a term of decency.
10. Not guilty.

WORD ORIGINS

Can you give the derivation of the following words?

1. Alphabet
2. Chortle
3. Quintessence
4. Tantalize
5. Bedlam
6. Sophomore
7. Piggyback
8. Pandemonium
9. Supercilious
10. Tawdry

WORD ORIGINS

1. It is simply a word combining the first two letters of the Greek alphabet—*alpha* and *beta*.

2. Meaning "to chuckle throatily." The word, a blend of "chuckle" and "snort," was coined by Lewis Carroll in the poem about the Jabberwock in *Through the Looking-Glass*.

3. The fifth essence which formed the basis of the stars. The Greeks added this to the four elements: earth, air, fire, and water.

4. Tantalize is derived from Tantalus, a king in Greek mythology, whom Zeus punished by immersing him in water with fine fruit above his head. When he tried to drink or eat, either the water receded or the fruit rose above his reach.

5. This is simply a contraction of St. Mary of Bethlehem, the name of an insane asylum in medieval London, and refers to the din made by the inmates.

6. One who is literally half wise and half foolish, from the Greek *sophos*, wise, and *moros*, foolish.

7. Originally pick-a-pack, similar to putting a knapsack on one's shoulders. When children were so carried, they changed the word to their own liking.

8. This is a word coined by John Milton in *Paradise Lost* for the capital of Hell. He formed it from the Greek *pan*, all, and *daimon*, demon. It passed into general use from the idea that Hell is a place of uproar and wild confusion.

9. "Supercilious" is a word characterized by scorn or disdain and is often accompanied by a raising of the eyebrows, which is how the word came about: from the Latin *super*, above, and *cilium*, eyelid.

10. From St. Audrey, on whose feast day the English sold cheap laces of such poor quality that the word tawdry passed into the language.

WORLD LITERATURE

1. In which language did Marcus Aurelius write?
2. A Maecenas is a munificent patron of literature or art. Of whom was the first Maecenas a patron?
3. In which novel did Raskolnikov play a leading part?
4. At whom did Émile Zola point the finger in *J'accuse*, and on whose behalf was he writing?
5. What is the *Book of Kells*, and where may it be seen?
6. Who wrote *Ghosts* and *Hedda Gabler*?
7. What did two famous Japanese novelists, Yasunari Kawabata and Yukio Mishima, have in common?
8. Which work of a world leader is reported to have sold over 800,000,000 copies?
9. How many stories are there in the *Decameron*, and who was the author?
10. In which classic work of literature would you find many such common expressions as the following:

   Mum's the word
   Wild goose chase
   Turn over a new leaf
   Every dog has its day
   Without a wink of sleep
   A finger in every pie
   Honesty's the best policy
   Birds of a feather flock together
   Earned with the sweat of my brows
   The proof of the pudding is in the eating

WORLD LITERATURE

1. Greek.
2. Horace and Virgil.
3. *Crime and Punishment*, by Fyodor Dostoyevsky.
4. The French General Staff. Captain Alfred Dreyfus, who was convicted of treason.
5. It is a beautifully illuminated manuscript of the Latin Gospels, dating from the eighth century, and is generally regarded as the finest example of Celtic illumination. It is one of the treasures of Trinity College Library in Dublin.
6. Henrik Ibsen, Norwegian dramatist and poet.
7. They both committed suicide: Kawabata by gas, and Mishima by *seppuku*, commonly called *hara-kiri*, or belly-slitting, which is considered honorable suicide by the Japanese.
8. *Quotations from the Works of Mao Tse-tung*.
9. The *Decameron*, by Giovanni Boccaccio, is a collection of one hundred witty and occasionally licentious tales set against the somber background of the Black Death.
10. *Don Quixote*, by Miguel de Cervantes, in the translation by Peter Motteux (1660-1718), an Anglo-French editor noted also for his translations of Rabelais. From *Don Quixote* we get the word "quixotic," which means striving with lofty enthusiasm for visionary ideals.

WORLD WAR II

1. On September 3, 1939, two days after World War II began, the signal "Winston is back" was flashed to all ship and bases of the Royal Navy. What did this signify?

2. In the early part of the war, during England's darkest hours, President Roosevelt sent a note to Prime Minister Churchill quoting some lines from Longfellow and adding, "I think this verse applies to your people as it does to us." What were the lines?

3. The battle of El Alamein was one of the turning points in the war. In what country did it take place, and who were the opposing commanders?

4. Who, according to the British, was "overpaid, oversexed and over here"?

5. What major operations had the code names Barbarossa and Overlord?

6. Which battle in the Pacific is considered to be one of the decisive Allied victories of the war?

7. Describe "Pluto" and the "Mulberries," which were used to great advantage during the Normandy landings.

8. In the United Kingdom, who was in command of Combined Operations, which carried out daring commando raids on the enemy throughout the war?

9. Can you translate the word *kamikaze*, the name given to the suicidal crash-attack planes used in desperation by the Japanese at the end of the war?

10. Which Allied general spurred his troops on in the following terms? "The quickest way to get it over with is to go get the bastards. . . . There's one thing you'll be able to say when you do go home. When you're sitting around your fireside with your brat on your knee, and he asks you what you did in the great World War II, you won't have to say you shoveled shit in Louisiana."

271

WORLD WAR II

1. That Prime Minister Chamberlain had appointed Winston Churchill First Lord of the Admiralty, the same position he held at the outbreak of World War I.
2. Sail on, O Ship of State
   Sail on, O Union, strong and great!
   Humanity with all its fears,
   With all the hopes of future years,
   Is hanging breathless on thy fate!
3. The western Egyptian desert. Rommel and Montgomery.
4. The American G.I. in Great Britain.
5. Barbarossa was the German invasion of Russia in 1941 (Frederick I of Germany was called this because of his red beard). Overlord stood for the Allied landings in Normandy in 1944.
6. The Battle of Midway, in 1942, which was fought chiefly with aircraft, resulted in the destruction of three Japanese aircraft carriers, crippling the Japanese navy.
7. "Pluto" was the code name for the submarine pipelines for oil. "Mulberries" were large synthetic harbors built on the beach which enabled ships to unload a vast amount of supplies before the major French Channel ports had been captured.
8. Vice-Admiral Lord Louis Mountbatten, whose father changed the family name from Battenberg during World War I.
9. Divine Wind, after the wind that had destroyed a Chinese armada in the thirteenth century.
10. General George S. Patton, Jr., in a speech to the troops of the Third Army in July 1944.

X-RATED

1. How did *X* come into being as a symbol for an unknown quantity?
2. What was the name of King Arthur's sword?-
3. Xerox, the trademark for a photocopying process, is derived from what?
4. Who was Xerxes?
5. Define xenophobia.
6. In the verse from Longfellow below what was the "strange device"?

    The shades of night were falling fast,
    As through an Alpine village passed
    A youth who bore, 'mid snow and ice,
    A banner with the strange device—

7. *Ex post facto* laws are specifically forbidden by the U.S. Constitution. Can you explain the reason for this?
8. Which Latin band leader is often photographed with a Chihuahua under his arm?
9. Who was Xanthippe?
10. What was the mysterious XYZ affair that caused such a stir in 1797-8?

X-RATED

1. It came into Europe from Arabia, where the word *shei*, meaning "thing," was used for an unknown quantity. This was transcribed as *xei* and later simplified to *X*. A famous example are X-rays, which were so named by their discoverer, Röntgen, because he did not understand their nature.

2. Excalibur.

3. Xerography, a dry photocopying process, from the Greek *xeros*, meaning dry, and *graphos*, written.

4. He was the king of Persia who, in the fifth century B.C., defeated Leonidas at Thermopylae and went on to pillage Athens.

5. Fear or hatred of strangers or foreigners.

6. A banner on which was written the single word "Excelsior!"

7. It insures that a person cannot be charged with breaking a law if the law was passed after the commission of the deed. *Ex post facto* means after the fact, or retroactive.

8. Xavier Cugat. (A Chihuahua is a very small dog named after a Mexican state.)

9. Socrates' wife, whose name is synonymous with a conjugal scold. Shakespeare refers to her in *The Taming of the Shrew*.

10. To settle a number of grievances against France, which included the taking of American ships by French privateers, President John Adams sent Gerry, Marshall, and Pinckney to Paris, where they met with three agents of Talleyrand, who were later identified to Congress as X, Y, and Z. These agents demanded a $50,000 payment to Talleyrand before any discussion could take place. This was refused, with Pinckney saying, "No, no, not a sixpence." All arguments were finally settled in 1800.

YIDDISH

Can you give the English equivalent of the following?

1. *Shlemiel*
2. *Shlimazel*
3. *Chutzpah*
4. *Megillah*
5. *Goy*
6. *Meshuga*
7. *Shmaltz*
8. *Nebbish*
9. *Shiksa*
10. *Shalom*

YIDDISH

1. A fool or clumsy bungler; one who spills the soup.
2. An even bigger fool, a luckless person; one on whom the shlemiel spills the soup.
3. Brazenness, unmitigated gall. One who kills his parents and asks for mercy on the grounds that he is an orphan has chutzpah.
4. A long complex story or explanation.
5. A Gentile.
6. Crazy.
7. Literally, cooking fat; excessive sentimentality.
8. A weak, helpless, or pathetic person.
9. Literally, an abomination; a non-Jewish girl; also implies an impious or wild Jewish girl.
10. Peace; hello; good-by.

ZEDS

1. What is a zed?
2. Name a leading symphony conductor who is a Parsee.
3. What does the acronym "Zip," as in Zip Code, mean?
4. Who was the ravishing and bubble-headed creature that captured the young Duke of Dorset's heart during Eights Week at Oxford?
5. What and where is the Isle of Cloves?
6. Within ten degrees, can you give the Celsius equivalent of absolute zero?
7. "Zounds" is a euphemism for which expression?
8. Who was married to the spokesman of the "lost generation"?
9. What was the name of the Jewish sect who died heroically defending the mountain fortress of Masada against the Tenth Roman Legion in A.D. 73?
10. Where is the point on the earth at 0° latitude, 0° longitude, and zero altitude?

ZEDS

1. The letter *z* in Great Britain. As Shakespeare said in *King Lear,* "Thou whoreson zed! Thou unnecessary letter!"
2. Zubin Mehta.
3. Zone Improvement Program.
4. Zuleika Dobson, in Max Beerbohm's novel of that name.
5. Zanzibar, off the coast of Tanzania. It supplies the bulk of the world demand for cloves.
6. 273° C.
7. God's wounds.
8. Zelda, the wife of F. Scott Fitzgerald.
9. The Zealots.
10. On the equator, in the Gulf of Guinea, off Ghana in west Africa.

ENDINGS

1. At what famous moment in history did who say? "*Voilà le commencement de la fin*"? (This is the beginning of the end.)
2. According to T.S. Eliot in "The Hollow Men," how does the world end?
3. The tune of "Till the End of Time" is based on which masterwork?
4. Which novel ends as follows: "John Thomas says good night to Lady Jane, a little droopingly, but with hopeful heart"?
5. What is the meaning of eschatology?
6. "Great is the art of beginning, but greater the art of ending" was written by which noted American poet?
7. Who said and in what work: "Laughter is not at all a bad beginning for a friendship, and it is far the best ending for one"?
8. Can you give the last two lines of the song "Taking a Chance on Love"?
9. Why does the word "penultimate" belong here?
10. To cover an awkward moment when the curtain failed to come down, which famous actress ad-libbed: "That's all there is. There isn't any more."?

ENDINGS

1. Talleyrand, on the announcement of Napoleon's Pyrrhic victory at Borodino in 1812.
2. "Not with a bang but a whimper."
3. Chopin's "Polonaise in A Flat."
4. *Lady Chatterley's Lover* by D.H. Lawrence.
5. The doctrine of last or final matters, such as death, resurrection, immortality, judgment.
6. Longfellow, "Elegiac Verse."
7. Oscar Wilde, in *The Picture of Dorian Gray*.
8. "We'll have a happy ending now,
   Taking a chance on love."
9. Because it means "next to last" (Latin *paene*, almost and *ultimus*, last).
10. Ethel Barrymore.